KEY MATHS

Intermediate

▶ Chris Humble
▶ Fiona McGill

© Paul Hogan, Chris Humble, Barbara Job, Fiona McGill 2001

The right of Paul Hogan, Chris Humble, Barbara Job and Fiona McGill to be identified as authors of this work has been asserted in accordance with the Copyright, Designs and Patents Act 1988.

All rights reserved. No part of this publication may be reproduced or transmitted in any form or by any means, electronic or mechanical, including photocopy, recording, or any information storage and retrieval system, without permission in writing from the publisher or under licence from the Copyright Licensing Agency Limited. Further details of such licences (for reprographic reproduction) may be obtained from the Copyright Licensing Agency Limited, of 90 Tottenham Court Road, London W1T 4LP.

First published in 2001 by
Nelson Thornes Limited
Delta Place
27 Bath Road
Cheltenham GL53 7TH

01 02 03 04 05 / 10 9 8 7 6 5 4 3 2 1

A catalogue record for this book is available from the British Library.

ISBN 0-7487-3395-7

The authors are grateful to the following examinations boards for permission to reproduce questions from their past examination papers. (Answers included have not been provided by the examining boards, they are the sole responsibility of the authors and may not necessarily constitute the only possible solutions.)

London Examinations, a division of Edexcel Foundation (UCLEAC/Edexcel)
Northern Examinations and Assessment Board (NEAB)
Associated Examining Board (SEG)
Welsh Joint Education Committee (WJEC)

The publishers have made every effort to contact copyright holders but apologise if any have been overlooked.

Artwork by Oxford Designers and Illustrators
Cartoons by Clinton Banbury
Typeset by Wyvern 21 Ltd, Bristol, UK
Printed and bound in Spain by Graficas Estella S.A.

Contents

Introduction iv

1 Number 1

Number skills 2
Types of number 6
Negative numbers 8
Ratio 10
Fractions, decimals and percentages 12
Using percentages 17
Indices 21
Practice questions 24

2 Algebra 25

Patterns in numbers 26
Use of algebra 28
Graphs of straight lines 31
Practical graphs 34
Solving equations 37
Curved graphs 40
Inequalities 44
Practice questions 47

3 Shape and space 51

Transformations 52
Trigonometry 56
Units of measurement 58
Perimeter and circumference 60
Pythagoras 62
Areas, nets and surface areas 64
Angles 68
Volume 72
Dimensional analysis 74
Symmetry 75
Loci 76
Practice questions 78

4 Handling data 79

Dealing with data 80
Averages 85
Comparing data 88
Simple probability 91
Laws of probability 94
Tree diagrams 95
Practice questions 98

Answers 100

Introducton

Key Maths GCSE Intermediate Revision Book has been developed as an invaluable revision resource for thorough preparation for Intermediate GCSE. Written by experienced authors with years of classroom experience, this book supports and enhances work done with the **Key Maths Intermediate GCSE Pupil Book**.

A number of features are included to help you with your intermediate revision and preparation.

- Each separate section covers the four core areas of the National Curriculum for Number, Algebra, Shape, space and measures and Handling data.

- Each section has an opening page identifying the key areas to be covered for ease of use.

- Every page comprehensively covers the key areas you need to study and revise. A notes section provides additional support and reminders where appropriate.

- Chapter 13 pages 301–305 These are provided to indicate where a particular topic is covered in the main pupil book. You can use this to refer back to the particular unit and page number in the pupil book.

- See also These show you where related or additional material is available within this book for extra practice.

- Test Yourself questions are provided after coverage of each core topic. These allow you to practise and gain confidence as you work through the book.

- At the end of each main section there are a range of actual examination questions for you to try. These allow you to test your understanding for each of the four core areas.

  Revision books for Foundation (ISBN: 0 7487 3394 9) and Higher (ISBN: 0 7487 3396 5) are also available.

Visit our extensive website at **www.nelsonthornes.com** for additional mathematics resources and materials to support your work.

1 Number

- [ ] **Number skills**
- [ ] **Types of number**
- [ ] **Negative numbers**
- [ ] **Ratio**
- [ ] **Fractions, decimals and percentages**
- [ ] **Using percentages**
- [ ] **Indices**

Practice questions

Number skills

☐ Place value with whole numbers

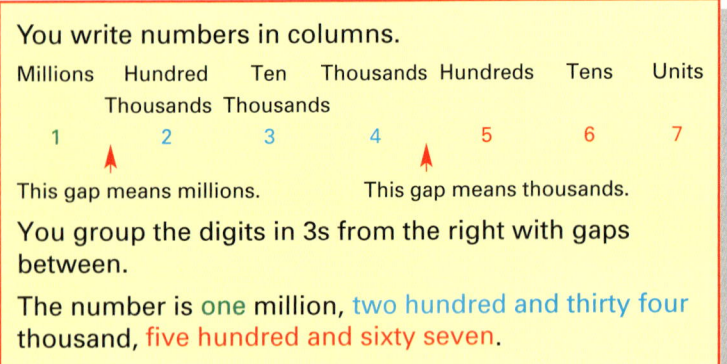

You write numbers in columns.

Millions	Hundred Thousands	Ten Thousands	Thousands	Hundreds	Tens	Units
1	2	3	4	5	6	7

This gap means millions. This gap means thousands.

You group the digits in 3s from the right with gaps between.

The number is one million, two hundred and thirty four thousand, five hundred and sixty seven.

The values get bigger as you go to the left.

☐ Place value with decimals

You need to remember the name for each place value.

Units	Tenths	Hundredths	Thousandths
7 .	6	5	4

The values get bigger as you go to the left.

10 tenths make a unit.
10 hundredths make a tenth.
10 thousands make a hundredth.

☐ Putting numbers in order of size

To put numbers in order of size, look at one place at a time.
Look at the numbers before the decimal point first.
Keep going to the right until a pair of digits differs.

Example

Put these numbers in order of size. Start with the smallest.
2.392, 2.329, 2.356

These are 2.3**2**9, 2.3**5**6, 2.3**9**2 in order.

Look at the second number after the decimal point. This is the first place the digits are all different.

☐ Multiplying and dividing by 10, 100 or 1000

To × by 10, move all the digits one column to the left.
To × by 100, move all the digits two columns to the left.
To × by 1000, move all the digits three columns to the left.

To ÷ by 10, move all the digits one column to the right.
To ÷ by 100, move all the digits two columns to the right.
To ÷ by 1000, move all the digits three columns to the right.

To × by 10 000 move 4 columns left,
to × by 100 000 move 5 columns left,
to × by 1 000 000 move 6 columns left,
and so on.

To ÷ by 10 000 move 4 columns right,
to ÷ by 100 000 move 5 columns right,
to ÷ by 1 000 000 move 6 columns right,
and so on.

Examples

Work out: **a** 62.3 × 100   **b** 249 ÷ 1000

	TTh	Th	H	T	U	.	t	h	th
		■	■	6	2	.	3		
× 100 gives			6	2	3	.	0		
			2	4	9	.			
÷ 1000 gives					0	.	■	■	■
					0	.	2	4	9

The blue squares show how many columns the digits have moved to the left.

The green squares show how many columns the digits have moved to the right.

☐ Adding, subtracting and dividing with decimals

When you do this: (1) Keep the decimal points in line.
(2) Fill any gaps with zeros.

Examples
Work out: **a** 2.45 + 3.7   **b** 4.7 − 0.32   **c** £73 ÷ 5

a
```
  2.45
+ 3.70 ←
  ————
  6.15
  1
```

b
```
  4.⁶7¹0 ←
− 0.32
  ————
  4.38
```

c
```
        14.6
     —————————
   5 ) 7 3 . ³0 0̸
                ↑
```

Notes

Follow the normal rules for addition, subtraction and division.
The arrows show the gaps that need to be filled with zeros.

☐ Multiplying decimals

The number of decimal places in the question is the same as in the answer.

To work out 6.4 × 27.3 do:

There are two decimal places in the question so there are two in the answer.

```
     27.3
  ×   6.4
  ——————
    10.92
   163.80
  ——————
   174.72
```

This is a long multiplication which is why there are three lines of working.
Remember to count the decimal places in the answer from the right.

When you work on the sum ignore the decimal points and treat it as 273 × 64.
Remember to do this you would need to do
$$273 \times 4 = 1092$$
then add on to it $263 \times 60 = 16380$
to get $273 \times 64 = 17472$

☐ Long division

To do long division, you need to work out some times tables for the number you divide by. To do 840 ÷ 24:

```
        3 5
     ————————
  24 ) 8 4 0
       7 2 ↓
       ———
       1 2 0
       1 2 0
       —————
       0 0 0
```

First do 84 ÷ 24.
Try 3 × 24 = 72 ✓ or 4 × 24 = 96 ✗
so 84 ÷ 24 = 3 and 84 − 72 = 12
Put the 3 above the 4 and bring down the 0
Now do 120 ÷ 24
Try 5 × 24 = 120 ✓ or 6 × 24 = 144 ✗
Put the 5 above the zero
and do 120 − 120

To do this you need to work out the 24 times table:
1 × 24 = 24
2 × 24 = 48
3 × 24 = 72
4 × 24 = 96
5 × 24 = 120
6 × 24 = 144

☐ BODMAS

Calculations must always be done in the same order.

First do	then	next do	and	then	and
B	**O**	**D**	**M**	**A**	**S**
Brackets	Powers of	Divide	Multiply	Add	Subtract

When two things have equal priority like × and ÷ you must work from left to right.

In $71.04 - 4.8^2$ the line acts like
$$2^3 \times \sqrt{9}$$
brackets on the top and bottom to give
$(71.04 - 4.8^2) \div (2^3 \times \sqrt{9})$

TEST YOURSELF

1 Write these numbers in words.
  a 9 070 501   **b** 70 400 076

2 Work these out.
  a 246.89 kg + 40.09 kg + 0.056 kg
  b 5.64 m − 2.968 m
  c 3.67 × 1.2
  d 396 ÷ 8

3 Work out:
  a 247 × 8.9   **b** 1355 ÷ 24

4 Work these out.
  a 6 ÷ 3 × 2
  b 24 − 8 ÷ 4
  c 3 + 2 × 4 − 3
  d 34 + 16²
  e 200 − 14²
  f 25² − 8³
  g 32 × (3⁵ − 214)   **h** $\dfrac{468.81 - 5.1^2 + 8}{\sqrt{196} \times 2.3}$

3

☐ Rounding numbers to the nearest 10, 100, 1000

> Numbers less than half way are always rounded down.
> Numbers that are half way are always rounded up.
> Numbers more than half way are always rounded up.

Examples
Round each of the areas **a** 4096 m² **b** 4500 m² **c** 4821 m² to the nearest 1000 m².

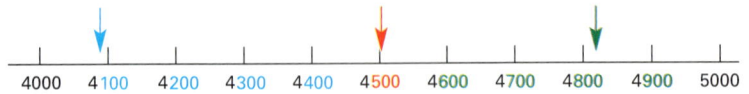

4096 m² is 4000 m²   4500 m² is 5000 m²   4821 m² is 5000 m²

☐ Rounding to any number of decimal places

> - Count out the number of decimal places, draw a line.
> - Look at the next digit. If it is 5, 6, 7, 8 or 9 add 1 to the last digit you keep. If it is 0, 1, 2, 3, or 4 leave it.
> - Cover any irrelevant figures with your finger.

☐ Rounding to any number of significant figures

> To do this you:
> - look at the first unwanted digit
> - if it is 5, 6, 7, 8 or 9 add one on to the digit you keep, if it is 0, 1, 2, 3 or 4 ignore it
> - keep the number about the right size.

Examples
Round these numbers:

a 45 to 1 sf   **b** 35 684 to 2 sf   **c** 0.7227 to 3 sf

a 45 to 1 sf is 50.
It is <u>not</u> 5!

b 35 684 to 2 sf is 36 000. It is not 36.

c 0.7227 to 3 sf is 0.723.

☐ Estimating

> To do this you round each number to 1 significant figure or a sensible estimate.

Examples
Estimate: **a** 8.7×6.3 **b** 250×15 **c** $4096 \div 769$ **d** $\sqrt{\dfrac{58 \times 79}{62}}$

a $8.7 \times 6.3 \approx 9 \times 6 = 54$ (calculator value 54.81)

b $250 \times 15 \approx 200 \times 20 = 4000$ (calculator value 3750)

c $4096 \div 769 \approx 4000 \div 800 = 40 \div 8 = 5$ (calculator value 5.3 to 1dp)

d $\sqrt{\dfrac{58 \times 79}{62}} \approx \sqrt{\dfrac{60 \times 80}{60}} = \sqrt{80} \approx \sqrt{81} = 9$ (calculator value 8.6 to 1dp)

Notes

The blue numbers are less than half way. The green numbers are more than half way. 4500 is exactly half way between 4000 and 5000.

Whatever the units, the same rules of rounding apply.

This calculator display $\boxed{56.48164379}$

becomes 56.4 | 8

which gives 56.5 to 1 decimal place.

Use the same rules of rounding for 2 or more decimal places. So here this display would be: 56.48 to 2 decimal places,
56.482 to 3 decimal places,
56.4816 to 4 decimal places.

Significant figures are normally abbreviated to sf.

This is one of the most common mistakes when finding significant figures.

35 684 could be a typical Premier League football attendance. But it is obvious that there would be roughly 36 000 at the game not 36!

$\approx$ means 'is roughly' or 'is approximately'.

Sometimes you need to use common sense and round so that you get a sensible estimate.
Rounding one number up and one number down gives a better estimate here.
To estimate a square root pick the nearest exact square and use its square root. Here 81 is the nearest exact square to 80.

4

Using an inverse to check a calculation

You can also check your answers by reversing the problem.
If you work out 765 × 32 the answer is 24 480.
The reverse of × is ÷. So you check by dividing.
You can work out 24 480 ÷ 32. You should get 765.

Error

Error is the difference between an exact answer and an estimate.

Error bounds

Take a number like 7 to the nearest whole number.

```
|    |    |    |    |    |    |    |    |    |
6.5  6.6  6.7  6.8  6.9  7.0  7.1  7.2  7.3  7.4  7.5
```

6.5 is the least number that would round up to 7.
7.49̇ is the greatest number that would round down to 7.
For the number 7, lower bound = 6.5 and upper bound = 7.5

In general if you want to find these do the following:

lower bound: take half the place value of the accuracy away
upper bound: add on half the place value of the accuracy.

Notes

To check an addition you would do a subtraction. So to check 479 + 567 = 1046 try 1046 − 567 or 1046 − 479.

You can check a sum by doing the opposite. So to check ÷ do × and to check − do +, etc.

Always make the error positive by taking the smaller number from the bigger number.

Percentage error = $\frac{\text{error}}{\text{exact answer}} \times 100$

Chapter 28 pages 193–195

You can write 7.4999... as 7.49̇.

But 7.49̇ is an awkward number to use so use 7.5 instead.

Edexcel refers to these as **greatest lower bound** and **least upper bound**.

Examples

Give the lower and upper bounds for each of these numbers.
a 760   which is correct to the nearest ten
b 9.2   which is correct to 1 dp
c 5400   which is correct to 2 sf

a Half the place value of ten is 5.
   lower bound = 755   upper bound = 765
b Half the place value of the first decimal place = 0.05
   lower bound = 9.15   upper bound = 9.25
c The place value of the 2nd significant figure is hundreds. Half of this is 50.
   lower bound = 5350   upper bound = 5450

Chapter 28 pages 196–201

TEST YOURSELF

1 Round these numbers:
(1) to the nearest 10   (2) to the nearest 1000.
a 1259   **b** 4460   **c** 5454   **d** 9898

2 Round these masses to 2 decimal places.
a 68.415 g   **b** 4.373 t   **c** 0.094 099 kg

3 Round these numbers:
a 0.069 91 to 3 sf   **b** 54 678 to 2 sf

4 Work these out. Do an estimate for each one.
a 7.6 × 4.2   **c** 7.6 + 9.2   **e** 48 × 674
b 283 ÷ 39   **d** 8.91 − 2.63   **f** 8352 ÷ 187

5 Give the upper and lower bounds of:
a 12.65 cm (to 2 dp)   **b** 17.379 02 km (to 5 dp)

6 Find **a** the error **b** the percentage error for an exact answer of 7.2 and an estimate of 8.

Types of number

☐ Even numbers and odd numbers

Some sets of numbers follow rules. These are sequences.
The even numbers and odd numbers are sequences.
Some patterns of shapes are shown for both.

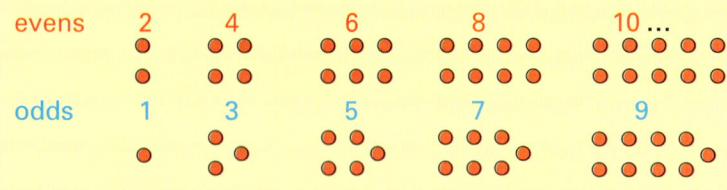

☐ Multiples

These are simply times tables. They are also sequences.
The multiples of 3 are   3   6   9   12   15….
which are the 3 times table 1×3 2×3 3×3 4×3 5×3…

See also ▶ **Patterns** page 26

☐ Common multiples

Here are the multiples of 3 and the multiples of 4.
3   6   9   **12**   15…   They have their lowest common
4   8   **12**   16   20…   multiple at 12. The next is 24.

☐ Factors

You can divide these exactly into another number.
These are all the factors of 24. They can be written out like this so you don't miss any.
    24   12   8   6
    1   2   3   4
So the factors of 24 are   1, 2, 3, 4, 6, 8, 12, 24.

☐ Prime numbers

These only divide by themselves and 1, so they have only two factors. 1 itself is **not** a prime number. It only has one factor.
The first eight prime numbers are 2, 3, 5, 7, 11, 13, 17, 19.
2 is the *only* even prime number.

☐ Prime factors

Look at factors of 24. Only 2 and 3 are prime numbers. This means they are the **prime factors** that divide into 24.

Notes

The rule for even numbers is add 2. These are also the multiples of 2. The dots… mean the sequence can go on forever…!
There are many patterns of shapes for evens e.g.

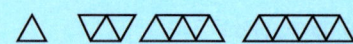

The rule for the odd numbers is also add 2 but these are not the multiples of two. There are different patterns for the odd numbers as well.

You can draw patterns for multiples.
  O   OOO   OOOO
  OO   OOO   OOOOO
The multiples of 7 are 7, 14, 21, 28, 35, …

You write each set of multiples out until you see the same number.
There are other common multiples of 3 and 4 e.g. 24, 36, 48, etc.

Sometimes the lowest common multiple is one of the numbers itself. For example, the lowest common multiple of 5 and 20 is 20.

Factors are always whole numbers.
The smallest number that goes into 24 is 1. The first pair you write down is 24 and 1. The next smallest number that goes in is 2. 2 goes in 12 times so you write down 12 and 2. You keep going like this until the factors 'cross over' $4 \times 6 = 24$ and $6 \times 4 = 24$ but you only need to write one 4 and one 6 down.

Prime numbers can only be shown by a rectangle with a width of 1, e.g. 7

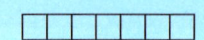

All other numbers can be shown as a rectangle where the width is more than 1. E.g. 15 is not a prime number because it can be shown like this   3

                                                                                          5

Writing a number as a product of its prime factors

Write 60 as a product of primes.
Divide by each prime number that will go in.
Start from 2. 60 ÷ 2 = 30. Put 30 underneath.
Try this same prime again. 30 ÷ 2 = 15.
You cannot divide 15 by 2, so try the
next biggest prime, which is 3. 15 ÷ 3 = 5
Finally 5 ÷ 5 = 1. You finish when you get to 1.
So 60 = 2 × 2 × 3 × 5

2	60
2	30
3	15
5	5
	1

Triangle numbers

The triangle numbers are a triangular pattern of shapes.
You can make them by adding the whole numbers together.

1   1 + 2   1 + 2 + 3   1 + 2 + 3 + 4   1 + 2 + 3 + 4 + 5

1   3   6   10   15 ...

Square numbers

You make these by multiplying numbers by themselves.

1 × 1   2 × 2   3 × 3   4 × 4   5 × 5

1   4   9   16   25...

You can also write them with an index (power).

1^2 2^2 3^2 4^2 5^2

Notes

Divide by the prime numbers in order of size.
Start with 2.
You can divide by the same prime more than once if it will go in.
You may prefer to use the factor tree method.
Here you break 60 into **any** two factors
(except 60 and 1!)
e.g. 60 = 3 × 20.
Look at these.
If either of them is a prime, circle and stop on that branch. Keep going until the bottom of every branch is circled.

Each pair of triangle number neighbours make a square number.

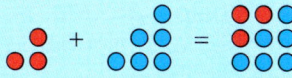

Chapter 4 pages 78–83

You should know your square numbers up to at least 10^2.

You can use the x^2 key on your calculator to find a square.

There are other patterns of shapes for square numbers.

You do the opposite of squaring to find a square root.
You can use the √ key on your calculator to find a square root.

TEST YOURSELF

1 Write down:
  a the multiples of 9 between 32 and 64
  b the common multiples of 3 and 5 up to 66
  c the lowest common multiple of 5 and 8
  d the lowest common multiple of 4, 6 and 9
  e the factors of 36
  f the product of prime factors for 72
  g the product of prime factors for 630
  h the triangle numbers between 20 and 50
  i the square numbers between 40 and 130

2 Look at these sets of numbers. Pick from this list the best words to describe them or fill the gap.
prime numbers, triangle numbers, multiples, factors, square, square root, even, odd.

  a 7, 11, 13, 17, 19   **f** 8, 10, 12, 14, 16
  b 9, 12, 15, 18, 21   **g** the ____ of 144 is 12
  c 6, 10, 15, 21, 28   **h** 51, 53, 55, 57, 59
  d 49, 64, 81, 100   **i** the ____ of 16 is 256
  e 1, 3, 6, 9, 18   **j** 1, 2, 4, 8, 16, 32

Negative numbers

☐ Putting numbers in order

Here are some bank balances: –£232, –£59, –£408, –£27
You can think of a number line to put them in order.

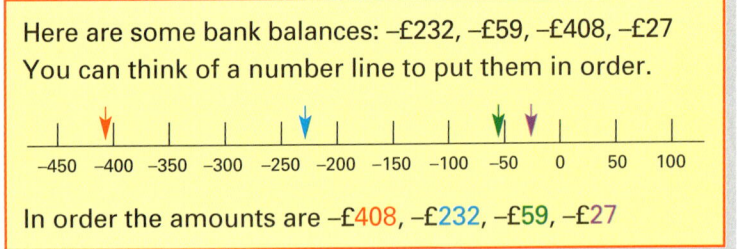

In order the amounts are –£408, –£232, –£59, –£27

Example

Doug works in tunnels. He starts 74 m underground, goes up 46 m then down 27 m. Find his new position.

You can write the first calculation like this –74 + 46
You can then sketch a number line to show you what to do.

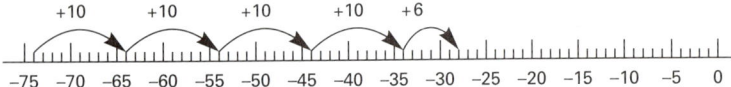

He is now 28 m below ground. So –74 + 46 = –28
You can write the next calculation like this –28 –27

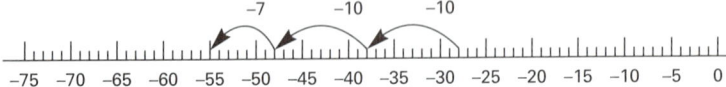

Doug is now 55 m below ground. So –28 –27 = –55

☐ Adding and subtracting with negative numbers

You can have two signs next to each other in calculations.

Mary owes £30 on one storecard and £25 on another.
She wants to know how much she owes.
You can write this as a calculation –£30 + –£25
You can see there are two signs together.
Think of amounts she has to pay out in £10 and £5 notes

–£10		–£10		–£10
–£10	+	–£10	=	–£10
–£10		–£5		–£10
				–£10
				–£10
				–£5

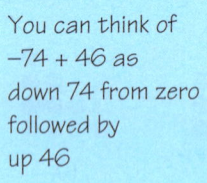

so –£30 + –£25 = –£55

Adding a negative number is the same as taking away.

Mary pays off £40 of the money she owes. You can think of this as taking money away from the amount she owes.

–£10		–£10		
–£10		–£10		
–£10	–	–£10		
–£10		–£10		
–£10			=	–£10
–£5				–£5

so – £55 – –£40 = –£15

Subtracting a negative number is the same as adding.

Notes

The further you go to the left on a number line, the less the numbers are.

The further you go to the right on a number line, the greater the numbers are.

On this number line –£27 is the most money and –£408 is the least.

The more negative a number is, the less it is. The closer to a positive number it is, the more it is.

The number line in the example is horizontal, but you can use a vertical one.

You can think of –74 + 46 as down 74 from zero followed by up 46

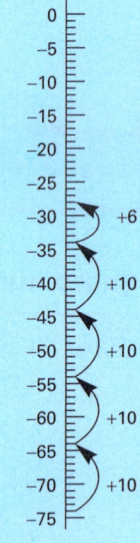

This shows + – together equal –

This shows – – together equal +

Rules for adding and subtracting negative numbers

These are the rules for 'double signs':

like signs give plus   unlike signs give minus

$$++ \atop --\} = +\qquad +- \atop -+\} = -$$

Examples

Work these out **a** 17+ –3 **b** 4 – –8 **c** –2 – +6 **d** –5 – –9

a 17 + –3 = 17 – 3 = 4

b 4 – –8 = 4 + 8 = 12

c –2 – +6 = –2 – 6 = –8

d –5 – –9 = –5 + 9 = 4

Rules for × and ÷ with negative numbers

These are exactly the same as for addition and subtraction

like signs give plus   unlike signs give minus

$$+\times+ \atop -\times-\}\ \ +\div+ \atop -\div-\} = +\qquad +\times- \atop -\times+\}\ \ +\div- \atop -\div+\} = -$$

Examples

Work these out **a** +5 × –6 **b** –24 ÷ –8

a +5 × –6 = –5 × 6 = –30

b –24 ÷ –8 = 24 ÷ 8 = 3

Rules for squaring and cubing negative numbers

Squaring a negative number always gives a positive.
Cubing a negative number always gives a negative.

Using negative numbers in formulas

Put the values of the letters in the formula.
Always remember to use BODMAS.

So to find $\dfrac{2a + 3b}{-6c}$ when $a = -12$, $b = -8$, $c = -4$,

do (2 × –12 + 3 × –8) ÷ (–6 × –4) = (–24 + –24) ÷ 24

= –48 ÷ +24 = –2

Notes

There are four possibilities with + and – together in 'double signs'. These are:

++   +–   –+   ––

Break each calculation into stages.
First do the double signs
then collect the numbers.

When you work out the green number calculations, you can go back to thinking of a number line.
So –5 + 9 becomes

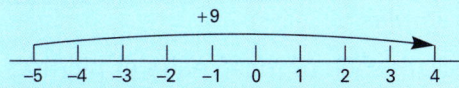

Chapter 5 pages 102–115

If a number doesn't have a sign in front of it, it is positive.
So 7 = +7

Break each sum into stages.
First do the double signs,
then multiply or divide.

–6 × –6 = +36 = 36
–5 × –5 × –5 = +25 × –5 = –125

You need to be prepared to use your calculator on problems like this. Make sure you know whether your calculator has a ± button or not. Some calculators will now enter a negative number if you key in e.g.

Others need you to key in 6 ± or ± 6

Within the first bracket, multiply first before adding.

TEST YOURSELF

1 Write these temperatures in order, from least to greatest.
–11 °C, –6 °C, 53 °C, –162 °C

2 Work these out. Show all your working.
- **a** –16 – 7
- **b** –1 + 3
- **c** 34 – 49
- **d** 7 + –4
- **e** –12 – +4
- **f** –14 – –9
- **g** –22 – 16
- **h** –19 + –28
- **i** –198 + –467

3 Work these out. Show all your working.
- **a** –6 × 3
- **b** –14 × –6
- **c** $(-6)^2$
- **d** 240 ÷ –30
- **e** $(-7)^3$
- **f** $(-2)^3 \div (-4)^2$

4 Work these out. Use $a = -4$, $b = -9$, $c = -2$.
- **a** $\dfrac{9a - 10b}{5c}$
- **b** $\dfrac{(-6c)^2 + ab}{2bc}$
- **c** $\dfrac{5.4a - 0.08b}{0.2c - a^3}$

Ratio

☐ Ratio

Look at these 2 piles of textbooks.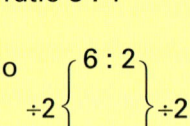
The first pile is three times
the height of the second one.
This means that their heights are in the ratio 3 : 1
Their numbers are in the ratio 6 : 2,
but you can divide both sides of the ratio
by 2

$$\div 2 \begin{Bmatrix} 6:2 \\ 3:1 \end{Bmatrix} \div 2$$

so the numbers are in the ratio 3 : 1

Examples

Look at each of these pairs of pictures.
For each one write down the ratio of their numbers.

a  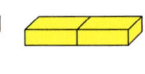   b

a The ratio is   8 : 2   b The ratio is   10 : 8
  which cancels to 4 : 1   which cancels to 5 : 4

☐ Expressing ratios in the form 1 : n or n : 1

For 1 : n, divide both sides by what gives you 1 on the left.
So in the form 1 : n, 10 : 28 = 10 ÷ 10 : 28 ÷ 10 = 1 : 2.8
For m : 1, divide both sides by what gives you 1 on the right.
So in the form m : 1, 8 : 5 = 8 ÷ 5 : 5 ÷ 5 = 1.6 : 1

☐ Sharing out using ratio

Look at this pile of cans.
Emma and Matt share them in the
ratio 3 : 2. How many does each get?
To do this question you need to find the number of shares.
There are 3 + 2 shares = 5 shares
There are 20 cans, so each share = 20 ÷ 5 = 4 cans
So Emma gets 3 × 4 = 12 cans and Matt gets
2 × 4 = 8 cans

Example
Peter is making some concrete. He mixes water, cement
and sand in the ratio 2 : 3 : 5. He has 126 kg of cement.
How much sand, water and concrete does he have?
3 shares = 126 kg   Each share = 126 ÷ 3 = 42 kg
So sand = 5 × 42 = 210 kg , water = 2 × 42 = 84 kg
2 + 3 + 5 = 10 shares, so concrete = 10 × 42 = 420 kg

Notes

Ratio is used to compare quantities.

If the piles were reversed they would be in the ratio 1 : 3

This is very like cancelling with fractions.

This is a situation where you may well need to use a calculator. So if you have to put 1.44 : 21.6 in the ratio 1: n
1.44 ÷ 1.44 = 1 and

| 2 | 1 | . | 6 | ÷ | 1 | . | 4 | 4 | = | 15 |

which gives 1 : 15

This means that for every 3 cans Emma has, Matt has 2

Every time Emma gets 3 cans Matt gets 2 so that 5 cans are given out altogether.

You can check if an answer is correct by adding the 2 shares to the 3 shares and the 5 shares. These should match the total weight of the concrete.
Here 84 kg + 126 kg + 210 kg = 420 kg which is the amount of concrete.

☐ Value for money

> Suppose you need to compare value for money for two items.
> To do this you work out the price for a fixed amount.

Example

Soup costs 38p for a 456 g can and 77p for a 847 g can. Which is better value?

You need to work out how many grams of soup you get for each penny.

456 ÷ 38 = 12 g per penny
847 ÷ 77 = 11 g per penny.

The 847 g can is better value. You get more grams per penny.

☐ Direct proportion

> Suppose bricks costs 20p each. So 1 brick costs 20p.
> Then 2 bricks cost 40p and 3 bricks cost 60p.
> In this situation the price increases at the same rate.
> This is called **direct proportion**.

Example

1 Here are the prices of some stamps.
   Fill in the gaps in this table marked with letters.

Amount	1	2	18	b
Cost	27p	54p	a	£5.94

a 18 stamps will cost 18 times as much as 1 stamp
   18 × 27 = £4.86
b Divide the cost by the cost for 1 stamp
   594 ÷ 27 = 22

2 12 apples cost £2.52. What is the cost of: **a** 8 apples **b** 27 apples?

a 1 apple costs £2.52 ÷ 12 = 21p
   8 apples cost 21 × 8 = £1.68
b 27 apples cost 21 × 27 = £5.67

Notes

A question might give you the masses of some cans as 400 g and 700 g.
Then it is best to find the price per 100 g.
You would divide the 400 g price by 4 and the 700 g price by 7.

Another question might give you the masses of some cans as 420 g and 760 g.
To compare them you could find the cost per 10 g.
You would divide the 420 g price by 42 and the 760 g price by 76.

If you plot a graph of numbers of bricks against cost, the points would lie on a straight line going through the origin.
The equation is $C = 20n$.

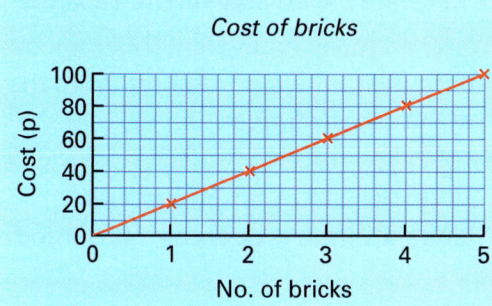

Cost of bricks

Make sure you divide with both costs in the same units. Here it is best to change both units into pence.

Chapter 7 pages 142–158

TEST YOURSELF

1 A large packet of grass seed has a mass of 45 kg. A smaller packet has a mass of 9 kg. What is the ratio of the big bag to the small bag?

2 A cereal is made by mixing oats, wheat and maize in the ratio 5 : 2 : 1. What mass of each is needed to make 248 kg of cereal?

3 Which pack of crisps is the best value: a 30 g pack for 36p or a 180 g pack for £1.98?

4 Which can of beans is the best value: a 224 g can for 19p or a 415 g can for 39p?

5 Fill in the gaps in this table marked with letters.

Number of rolls	1	2	4	8	c
Cost	16p	32p	a	b	£4.48

Fractions, decimals and percentages

☐ Improper fractions and mixed numbers

Examples **a** Write $2\frac{3}{4}$ as a top heavy fraction.
b Write $\frac{9}{2}$ as a mixed fraction.

a $2\frac{3}{4}$ looks like this  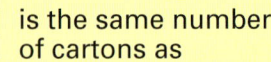 This is 11 quarters or $\frac{11}{4}$

b $\frac{9}{2}$ looks like this 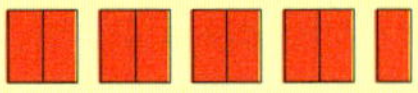 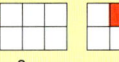 So it is $4\frac{1}{2}$

☐ Equivalent fractions

Look at these trays for 8 cartons of raspberries.
Each carton is $\frac{1}{8}$ of the tray.

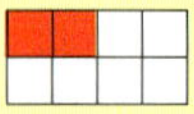

 is the same number of cartons as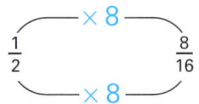

so $\frac{1}{2}$ = $\frac{2}{8}$ of a tray

These are called **equivalent** fractions.

You can make equivalent fractions by multiplying the top and bottom of the fraction by the same number.

Examples

Change **a** $\frac{1}{2}$ into sixteenths, **b** $\frac{4}{5}$ into hundredths

a

$\frac{1}{2}$ ⟶ $\frac{}{16}$ (× 8) $\frac{1}{2}$ ⟶ $\frac{8}{16}$ (× 8)

They are the **same** fraction shown in different ways.

b

$\frac{4}{5}$ ⟶ $\frac{1}{100}$ (× 20) $\frac{4}{5}$ ⟶ $\frac{80}{100}$ (× 20)

☐ Cancelling fractions

You can cancel fractions by **dividing**.
Look at the top and bottom of the fraction.
If they are are in the same times table you can divide both **by the same number**.

$\frac{4}{8}$ ⟶ $\frac{1}{2}$ (÷ 4)

Notes

An improper fraction is a top heavy fraction.

There is another way to do these.
With $2\frac{3}{4}$ there are 4 quarters in each of the 2 whole ones. Then add the 3 extras on. So $2 \times 4 + 3$ gives 11 quarters = $\frac{11}{4}$

There are 2 halves in each whole one. So divide the 9 by 2 to find how many whole ones. The one left over is the extra $\frac{1}{2}$.

You may find it helps to see the $\frac{1}{4}$ shown like this.

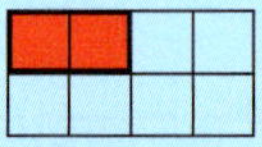

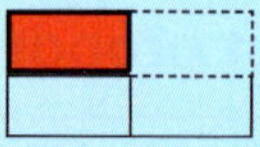

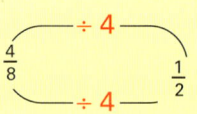

You can check these are the same on a calculator.

1 ÷ 4 = 0.25

2 ÷ 8 = 0.25

Equivalent fractions have the same value but are shown in different ways.

The top of a fraction is the numerator.

The bottom of a fraction is the denominator.

Chapter 9 pages 184–186

Here both 4 and 8 are in the 4 times table. So both 4 and 8 will divide by 4.

What you do to the top of a fraction, you must do to the bottom.

TEST YOURSELF

1 Write these as improper (top heavy) fractions.
a $1\frac{1}{2}$ **b** $2\frac{2}{3}$ **c** $3\frac{3}{4}$
d $3\frac{2}{5}$ **e** $4\frac{5}{6}$ **f** $4\frac{15}{16}$

2 Write these as mixed numbers.
a $\frac{5}{2}$ **b** $\frac{14}{3}$ **c** $\frac{15}{4}$
d $\frac{21}{5}$ **e** $\frac{21}{8}$ **f** $\frac{37}{12}$
g $\frac{22}{7}$ **h** $\frac{35}{9}$ **i** $\frac{45}{25}$

3 Make these fractions equivalent.
a $\frac{1}{2} = \frac{}{8}$ **b** $\frac{3}{8} = \frac{}{16}$ **c** $\frac{4}{5} = \frac{}{10}$
d $\frac{3}{7} = \frac{}{14}$ **e** $\frac{14}{25} = \frac{}{100}$ **f** $\frac{8}{9} = \frac{}{360}$

4 Cancel these fractions down.
a $\frac{2}{4}$ **b** $\frac{6}{8}$ **c** $\frac{10}{16}$
d $\frac{4}{16}$ **e** $\frac{3}{12}$ **f** $\frac{6}{9}$
g $\frac{5}{20}$ **h** $\frac{10}{25}$ **i** $\frac{8}{24}$

☐ Adding and subtracting fractions

To + or – fractions the denominators must be the same.
So $\frac{1}{8} + \frac{5}{8} = \frac{6}{8}$ and cancelling down $\frac{6}{8} = \frac{36}{48}$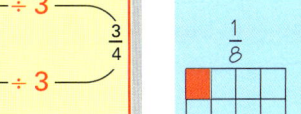

When the denominators in fractions are different, you must make the denominators the same.
You do this by finding equivalent fractions.

Notes

The bottom number is the denominator.

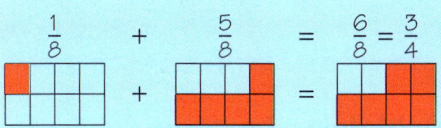

This is called finding the lowest common denominator.

Example $\frac{15}{16} - \frac{1}{8}$

First change $\frac{3}{4}$ into sixteenths.

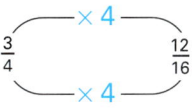

Then subtract as normal $\frac{15}{16} - \frac{12}{16} = \frac{3}{16}$

You add mixed numbers by adding the whole numbers first and then the fractions.
You subtract mixed numbers by making them improper.

You always multiply the top and bottom by the same number.
The lowest number 4 and 16 both divide into is 16.
So the lowest common denominator of 4 and 16 is 16.

5   10   15   20
4   8   12   16   20

The lowest number 5 and 4 both divide into is 20 (the lowest common denominator of 4 and 5 is 20).

So you make both $\frac{4}{5}$ and $\frac{3}{4}$ into twentieths.

Examples

a $1\frac{4}{5} + 5\frac{3}{4}$ **b** $2\frac{5}{6} - 1\frac{2}{3}$

a $1 + 5 = 6$ then $\frac{4}{5} + \frac{3}{4} = \frac{16}{20} + \frac{15}{20} = \frac{31}{20} = 1\frac{11}{20}$

Add these two answers $6 + 1\frac{11}{20} = 7\frac{11}{20}$

b $2\frac{5}{6} - 1\frac{2}{3} = \frac{17}{6} - \frac{5}{3}$
$= \frac{17}{6} - \frac{10}{6} = \frac{7}{6} = 1\frac{1}{6}$

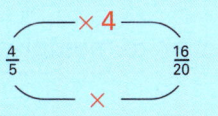   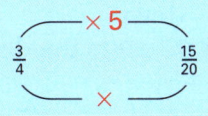

Chapter 9 pages 187–190 ▶

The top of a fraction is the numerator.
It tells you how many of the denominator there are.
So $\frac{4}{5}$ means there are 4 lots of $\frac{1}{5}$.

☐ Finding fractions of quantities

In the fraction, $\frac{3}{4}$ the top number is 3.
This means that there are 3 lots of $\frac{1}{4}$ in the number.
So to find $\frac{3}{4}$ of a number: (1) divide it by 4
                             (2) multiply by 3.

TEST YOURSELF

1 Work these out.

   a $\frac{2}{3}$ of 21   **b** $\frac{2}{3}$ of 36   **c** $\frac{3}{4}$ of 24
   d $\frac{2}{5}$ of 25   **e** $\frac{3}{5}$ of 50   **f** $\frac{4}{5}$ of 380
   g $\frac{5}{6}$ of 72   **h** $\frac{8}{9}$ of 756   **i** $\frac{4}{25}$ of 800

2 Work these out.

   a $\frac{1}{4} + \frac{1}{4}$ **b** $\frac{3}{4} - \frac{1}{4}$ **c** $\frac{5}{8} + \frac{7}{8}$
   d $\frac{13}{16} - \frac{3}{16}$ **e** $\frac{5}{6} + \frac{4}{6}$ **f** $\frac{4}{5} - \frac{1}{5}$
   g $\frac{6}{17} - \frac{4}{17}$ **h** $\frac{5}{8} + \frac{1}{8}$ **i** $\frac{5}{12} - \frac{1}{12}$

3 Work these out.

   a $\frac{3}{4} + \frac{1}{2}$ **b** $\frac{3}{4} - \frac{5}{16}$ **c** $\frac{5}{8} + \frac{7}{16}$
   d $\frac{3}{5} - \frac{3}{10}$ **e** $\frac{5}{6} + \frac{2}{3}$ **f** $\frac{4}{5} - \frac{3}{20}$
   g $\frac{3}{4} - \frac{7}{12}$ **h** $\frac{5}{2} + \frac{5}{8}$ **i** $\frac{5}{7} - \frac{4}{9}$

4 Work these out.

   a $2\frac{1}{4} + 1\frac{1}{2}$ **b** $3\frac{1}{2} - 1\frac{3}{16}$
   c $5\frac{1}{3} + 3\frac{5}{6}$ **d** $4\frac{4}{5} - 1\frac{3}{10}$
   e $6\frac{3}{4} + 2\frac{4}{5}$ **f** $7\frac{1}{7} - 5\frac{2}{3}$

☐ Ordering fractions

To find if $\frac{5}{8}$ is bigger than $\frac{3}{5}$ use equivalent fractions.
The lowest common denominator of 8 and 5 is 40.
$\frac{5}{8} = \frac{25}{40}$ $\frac{3}{5} = \frac{24}{40}$ so $\frac{5}{8}$ is bigger than $\frac{3}{5}$

Notes

5   10   15   20   25   30   35
8   16   24   32

☐ Multiplying fractions

To do this:
- Turn any mixed fractions to improper fractions.
- Write the sum out. Leave space for any working.
- **Cancel** if you can
- × **the tops** together then × **the bottoms** together
- Turn any improper fractions back to mixed fractions.

With a pair of fractions you can cancel in these directions (if it is possible).

Think of a butterfly to help you remember this.

So $\frac{\cancel{12}^3}{\cancel{25}_5} \times \frac{\cancel{5}^1}{\cancel{16}_4}$ cancels as shown.

Examples

Evaluate: **a** $\frac{5}{6} \times \frac{3}{4}$ **b** $3\frac{3}{4} \times 1\frac{7}{25}$

a $\frac{5}{\cancel{6}_2} \times \frac{\cancel{3}^1}{4} = \frac{5 \times 1}{2 \times 4} = \frac{5}{8}$

Evaluate means 'work these out'.

b $3\frac{3}{4} = \frac{15}{4}$ $1\frac{7}{25} = \frac{32}{25}$

$\frac{\cancel{15}^3}{\cancel{4}_1} \times \frac{\cancel{32}^8}{\cancel{25}_5} = \frac{3 \times 8}{1 \times 5} = \frac{24}{5} = 4\frac{4}{5}$

There are 3 lots of 5 in 15 and 5 lots of 5 in 25.
There is 1 lot of 4 in 4 and 8 lots of 4 in 32.

☐ Dividing fractions

- Turn the fraction after the division sign upside down.
- Change the divide sign to multiply.

Chapter 9 pages 191–192

Examples

Evaluate: **a** $\frac{5}{6} \div \frac{15}{16}$ **b** $4\frac{1}{2} \div 2\frac{7}{10}$

a $\frac{5}{6} \div \frac{15}{16} = \frac{\cancel{5}^1}{\cancel{6}_3} \times \frac{\cancel{16}^8}{\cancel{15}_3} = \frac{1 \times 8}{3 \times 3} = \frac{8}{9}$

There are 3 lots of 5 in 15 and 1 lot of 5 in 5.
There are 3 lots of 2 in 6 and 8 lot of 2 in 16.

b $4\frac{1}{2} = \frac{9}{2}$ $2\frac{7}{10} = \frac{27}{10}$

$\frac{9}{2} \div \frac{27}{10} = \frac{\cancel{9}^1}{\cancel{2}_1} \times \frac{\cancel{10}^5}{\cancel{27}_3} = \frac{1 \times 5}{1 \times 3} = \frac{5}{3} = 1\frac{2}{3}$

Remember to make the fractions improper before starting the calculation. This is the same for subtraction, multiplication and division.

TEST YOURSELF

1 Which is bigger $\frac{2}{3}$ or $\frac{5}{7}$?

2 Work these out.
  a $\frac{1}{2} \times \frac{4}{5}$ **b** $\frac{3}{8} \times \frac{2}{5}$ **c** $\frac{2}{3} \times \frac{9}{10}$
  d $\frac{3}{5} \div \frac{3}{10}$ **e** $\frac{7}{8} \div \frac{3}{4}$ **f** $\frac{3}{5} \div \frac{9}{20}$

3 Work these out.
  a $1\frac{1}{2} \times \frac{4}{5}$ **b** $2\frac{3}{4} \times 3\frac{1}{5}$ **c** $7\frac{1}{3} \times 1\frac{7}{8}$
  d $2\frac{3}{4} \times \frac{4}{11}$ **e** $4\frac{1}{6} \times 2\frac{1}{10}$ **f** $5\frac{4}{9} \times 4\frac{2}{7}$
  g $1\frac{1}{4} \div \frac{1}{8}$ **h** $1\frac{5}{6} \div 2\frac{2}{3}$ **i** $8\frac{1}{2} \div 4\frac{1}{4}$
  j $3\frac{1}{3} \div 2\frac{2}{9}$ **k** $5\frac{3}{5} \div 2\frac{1}{10}$ **l** $12\frac{1}{2} \div 1\frac{1}{8}$

☐ Writing percentages

> Percentages are just another way of writing hundredths.
> So you can write $\frac{7}{100}$ as 7% and $\frac{89}{100}$ as 89%
> Percentages add up to 100%.
> So if you spend 60% of your money there will be 40% left.

Example
June scores $\frac{68}{100}$ in an exam.
a Write this as a percentage.
b What percentage of the exam did she get wrong?

a She scored 68%   **b** 100% − 68% = 32%
                          She got 32% wrong.

☐ Changing fractions to decimals

> The line in a fraction means *divide*.
> So you can read $\frac{3}{4}$ like this: 3 divided by 4
>
> If you do this, you get a decimal $4 \overline{)3.\,^30\,^20}$
> 0. 7 5

Example
Change to a decimal: **a** $\frac{9}{20}$ **b** $\frac{5}{8}$

a $9 \div 20 = 20\overline{)9.\,^90\,^{10}0}$ **b** $8\overline{)5.\,^50\,^20\,^40}$
           0. 4 5   0. 6 2 5

☐ Changing decimals to percentages

> To change a decimal to a percentage, multiply by 100.

 **Multiplying and dividing by 100, 100 or 1000** page 2

Example
Change to a percentage: **a** 0.27   **b** 0.04
a 0.27 = 0.27 × 100% = 27%
b 0.04 = 0.04 × 100% = 4%

☐ Changing fractions to percentages

> To do this you need to combine the last two topics!
> (1) Change the fraction to a decimal.
> (2) Change the decimal to a percentage.

 **Equivalent fractions** page 12

Notes

This is 1%. It is 1 square out of 100.

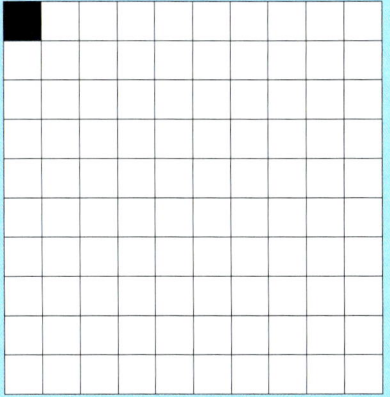

It is not very much!
That is because 1% = $\frac{1}{100}$

In the square above 1% is shaded.
This means that 99% isn't shaded.

You can do these on a calculator like this

9 ÷ 2 0 =   0.45
5 ÷ 8 =   0.625

This is because 100% = 1 whole one
so   1% = 1 ÷ 100 = 0.01
and   100% = 0.01 × 100 = 1

Some fractions can be changed to percentages by using equivalent fractions.

e.g. $\frac{22}{50} \xrightarrow{\times 2} \frac{44}{100} = 44\%$

15

Examples

Change to a percentage: **a** $\frac{7}{40}$ **b** $\frac{21}{26}$

a Step 1 $7 \div 40 = 0.175$
   Step 2 $0.175 \times 100 = 17.5\%$
b Step 1 $21 \div 26 = 0.8076....$
   Step 2 $0.8076... \times 100 = 80.76\% = 80.8\%$ (1dp)

Changing fractions to decimals

 **Place value with whole numbers** page 2

Example

Change to fractions: **a** 0.4 **b** 0.32 **c** 0.007

a The 4 here is in the *tenths* column.
So $0.4 = \frac{4}{10}$ then cancelling down gives $\frac{2}{5}$.

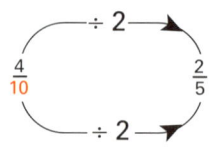

b The 2 is in the *hundredths* column, so you have to make a fraction over 100.
The fraction is $\frac{32}{100}$ then cancelling down gives $\frac{8}{25}$.

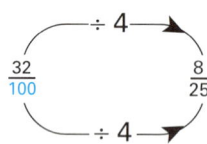

c The 7 is under the *thousandths* column so the fraction is $\frac{7}{1000}$. This cannot be cancelled.

Changing percentages to decimals

> The rule here is to divide by 100
> So 27% as a decimal = $27 \div 100 = 0.27$

Changing percentages to fractions

> 'Per cent' means out of 100 so put the percentage over 100. Then cancel down if you can.

Example

Change to a fraction. **a** 77% **b** 45%

a $77\% = \frac{77}{100}$

b $45\% = \frac{45}{100}$ then cancelling gives $\frac{9}{20}$.

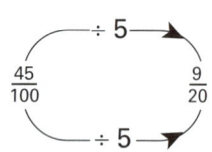

Notes

You may notice that $\frac{7}{40}$ is the rate, as a fraction, of VAT!

For this you need to remember your place value. You also need to be able to cancel down.

U	t	h	th
0 .	4		
0 .	3	2	
0 .	0	0	7

This is because 100% = 1 whole one
so 1% = $1 \div 100 = 0.01$
and 100% = $0.01 \times 100 = 1$

Chapter 9 pages 193–198

To divide by 100 move the digits 2 columns to the right.

H	T	U	t	h
	2	7		
	0 .	2	7	

No cancelling is possible with $\frac{77}{100}$

TEST YOURSELF

1 Change each of these to decimals.
a $\frac{3}{5}$ **b** $\frac{1}{4}$ **c** $\frac{2}{3}$ **d** $\frac{3}{8}$

2 Change each of these to percentages.
a 0.5 **b** 0.05 **c** 0.08 **d** 0.58

3 Change each of these to percentages.
a $\frac{2}{5}$ **b** $\frac{3}{4}$ **c** $\frac{7}{8}$ **d** $\frac{5}{7}$

4 Change each of these to decimals.
a 25% **b** 70% **c** 7% **d** 77%

5 Change each of these to fractions.
a 0.3 **b** 0.7 **c** 0.01 **d** 0.08
e 0.47 **f** 0.75 **g** 0.66 **h** 0.008

6 Change each of these to fractions.
a 25% **b** 40% **c** 65% **d** 24%

7 Match any cards that show the same amount.

0.42	0.04	$\frac{21}{50}$	$2\frac{1}{25}$	4%	21%	$\frac{21}{25}$
0.4	0.21	$\frac{2}{5}$	$\frac{1}{25}$	42%	40%	0.84

16

Using percentages

☐ **Finding a percentage of an amount**

> (1) Write the percentage as a decimal.
> (2) Multiply the quantity by the decimal.

Example
Mark earns 8% interest per year on his savings of £585.
Work out how much interest he has after 1 year.

8% = 0.08   0.08 is called the **multiplier** for finding 8%
then by hand
$$\begin{array}{r} 585 \\ \times\ 0.08 \\ \hline 46.80 \end{array} = £46.80$$

or if you can use a calculator then key in

| 0 | . | 0 | 8 | × | 5 | 8 | 5 | = | Answer £46.80

See also ▶ **Fractions** page 16   **VAT** page 18

Notes

With simple percentages you may find it easier to use fractions.
The percentages you should be able to use fractions with are:
50%   (finding a half)
25%, 75%,   (finding quarters)
10%, 30%, 70%, 90% (finding tenths)
20%, 40%, 60%, 80%, (finding fifths)
$33\frac{1}{3}$%, $66\frac{2}{3}$%,   (finding thirds).

Your calculator will display 46.8
Don't forget that it is money so you must write a zero on the end to give £46.80

Chapter 9 pages 191–200 ▶

☐ **Percentage increase and decrease**

> You can use a percentage to find an *increase* in an amount.
> The amount you start with is 100% so the multiplier will be more than 1.

Example
Bernard pays £450 for a mower. He sells it for 20% more than he bought it. Work out how much he sells it for.
You can find the multiplier like this:
100% + 20% = 120% = 1.2
then by long multiplication 450 × 1.2 = £540

or key in | 1 | . | 2 | × | 4 | 5 | 0 | = | Answer £540

> You can use a percentage to find a *decrease* in an amount.
> The amount you start with is 100% so the multiplier will be less than 1.

Example
Jo buys a motorbike for £2680.
She sells it for 24% less than this. How much does she get?

You can find the multiplier like this:
100% − 24% = 76% = 0.76
then by long multiplication £2680 × 0.76 = £2036.80

You start with 100% of £450. The increase is 20% of £450.
So you are trying to find
100% + 20% = 120% of £450

You can use a simpler but slower method.
First find 20% of £450 then add it to £450.
20% of £450 = 0.2 × 450 = £90
Then £450 + £90 = £540

You could do this by using fractions.
120% = $1\frac{1}{5}$ then $\frac{6}{5} \times \frac{450}{1}$ £540

Bernard has made a profit on this mower
A 20% gain is a 20% profit.
You may be asked to find the profit in a question. This will be an increase.

A decrease is the same as a reduction.
You can use a simpler but slower method.
First find 24% of £2680 then take it away from £2680.
24% of £2680 = 0.24 × 2680 = £643.20
Then £2680 − £643.20 = £2036.80

Jo has made a loss on this bike.
You may be asked to find the loss in a question. This will be a decrease.

TEST YOURSELF

1 Find the multiplier for:
  a an increase of 42%   **b** a loss of 36%

2 Find each of these.
  a 23% of £400   **b** 9% of £360

3 Find the new amounts after these changes.
  a 30% increase on £900
  b 24% profit on £4080
  c 36% loss on £2150
  d 4% reduction on £7360

☐ VAT

VAT is charged at 17.5%. This is also 10% + 5% + 2.5%.
So to find VAT   set it out like this
(1) Find a tenth to get   10% = ...
(2) halve this to find   5% = ...
(3) halve this to find   2.5% = ...
(4) add together   17.5% = _____

Example

A garage bill for an MOT is £80 + VAT.
a Find the VAT
b Find the total amount to pay.

a (1) 10% of £80 = $\frac{1}{10}$ of £80   = £8
   (2) 5% of £80 = $\frac{1}{2}$ of £8   = £4
   (3) 2.5% of £80 = $\frac{1}{2}$ of £4   = £2
   (4) Add it all together so 17.5% = £14
b £80 + £14 = £94

☐ Tax

Your **tax allowance** is the money you earn before paying tax.

Your **taxable income** = your **earnings** – your **tax allowance**.

Income tax is at three rates: 20%, 22% and 40%.

Example

Jerome earns £17 800 a year. His tax allowance is £5000.
He pays tax at 20% on the first £4300 of taxable income.
He pays tax at 22% on the rest.

a What is his taxable income?
b How much tax does he pay each month?

a His taxable income is £17 800 – £5000 = £12 800
b The first £4300 of taxable income is taxed at 20%.
   20% = 0.2 then 0.2 × £4300 = £860
   This leaves £12 800 – £4300 = £8500 to be taxed at 22%.
   23% = 0.22 then 0.22 × £8500 = £1870
   then he pays (£860 + £1870) ÷ 12 = £227.50 tax per month

Notes

VAT is Value Added Tax.

To find 10%, divide by 10.

The multiplier for VAT is 0.175.
The multiplier for increasing an amount by the VAT rate is 1.175.

You might prefer to do 10% = 0.1
Then 0.1 × £80 = £8

Chapter 9 page 201

With a calculator this is a lot easier!
17.5% = 17.5 ÷ 100 = 0.175

then 0 . 1 7 5 × 8 0 = £14

Earnings are the amount you are paid for the work you do.
Earnings are usually paid as either wages or as a salary.
Wages are usually paid weekly.
A salary is usually paid monthly.

Chapter 29 pages 217–220

Always round the final amount to the nearest penny, if it is not an exact answer.

TEST YOURSELF

1 Find the VAT on these amounts.
   a £100   **b** £60   **c** £250
2 Increase these amounts by adding on VAT.
   a £32   **b** £4500   **c** £965

3 Pippa earns £18 200 per year. Her tax allowance is £4200. She pays 20% tax on the first £4300 of taxable income and 22% on the rest.
   Find: **a** her taxable income
         b the tax she pays per month.

Expressing one number as a percentage of another

You have already seen that 7 out of 100 = $\frac{7}{100}$ = 7%

To change numbers to percentages you have to make them out of 100. With some numbers you can use equivalence.

Example

Change a score of 40 out of 50 to a percentage.

You can write this as a fraction: $\frac{40}{50}$

Then you can make it equivalent to a fraction out of 100,

 so 40 out of 50 = 80%

See also > **Fractions** page 16

Notes

This method is particularly useful where the bottom number in the fraction is one of the factors of 100.

1, 2, 4, 5, 10, 20, 25, 50, 100

To express one number as a percentage of another number sometimes you cannot use equivalent fractions.

Then you need to use these steps.

(1) Divide the first number by the second one.
(2) Multiply by 100.

This is when you cannot multiply the bottom number in a fraction to make 100.

An example is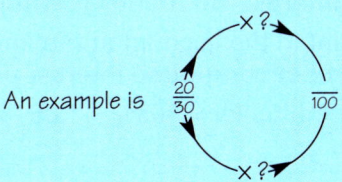

Examples

Find: **a** 3 as a percentage of 5
b 5 goals as a percentage of 16 shots.
c 35 kg as a percentage of 168 kg

a 3 ÷ 5 = 0.6   then 0.6 × 100 = 60
b 5 ÷ 16 = 0.3125   then 0.3125 × 100 = 31.25%
c 35 ÷ 168 = 0.2083…. then 0.2083… × 100 = 20.1% (1 dp)

You might be asked for an answer to 1 decimal place. If so, it would be 31.3%.

Percentage change

You can use the methods above to find percentage change.

Percentage change = $\frac{\text{actual change}}{\text{starting value}} \times 100\%$

You can use this method to find percentage profit, percentage loss and percentage error.

Percentage profit = $\frac{\text{profit}}{\text{starting value}} \times 100$

Percentage loss = $\frac{\text{loss}}{\text{starting value}} \times 100$

Percentage error = $\frac{\text{error}}{\text{starting value}} \times 100$

Examples

Find the percentage increase when a fare is increased from £8 to £10.

actual increase = £10 − £8 = £2   starting value = £8
Now find £2 as a percentage of £8.

2 ÷ 8 = 0.25   then 0.25 × 100 = 25%

Finding an interest rate

You can find the interest rate on an amount using this formula

Interest rate = $\frac{\text{actual interest}}{\text{starting value}} \times 100\%$

Example
Find the interest rate if £360 saved for 1 year becomes £380.
actual interest = £380 − £360 = £20   starting value = £360
Interest rate = $\frac{20}{360} \times 100\% = 5.6\%$ (1 dp)

Compound interest

To find the increase in an amount due to compound interest:
- Find the rate of compound interest as a multiplier.
- Multiply the amount by the multiplier as many times as the number of years the amount is invested.

Example
£900 is invested for 4 years. It earns 5% per annum compound interest. No money is withdrawn. Find:
a the amount in the account at the end of 4 years
b the amount of compound interest paid.
a Rate as a multiplier = 105% = 1.05
Amount = 900 × 1.05 × 1.05 × 1.05 × 1.05 = £1093.96
b Interest paid = £1093.96 − 900 = £193.96

Reverse percentage problems

Sometimes you need to undo a percentage change.
To do this you need to make the multiplier into a 'divider'

Example
Felicity sells a motorbike for £750 and makes a 20% profit. What did the motorbike originally cost her?
Original multiplier = 100% + 20% = 120% = 1.2

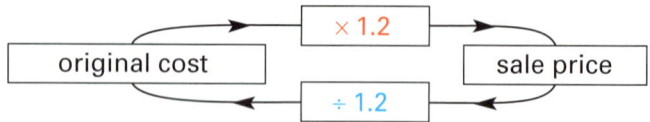

750 ÷ 1.2 = 625   So the original cost was £625

Notes

An interest rate is always given as a percentage.

For simple interest the interest in the second year is the same as in the first year.

For compound interest you earn more interest in the second year than in the first. This is because the first year interest is added and so earns interest as well as the original amount.

It is a lot quicker to multiply by a power of the multiplier.
Here it is $900 \times (1.05)^4 = £1093.96$

Chapter 29 page 220–222

These are often called 'finding the original cost' problems although they can involve quantities like distance, times, etc.
To 'undo' VAT, divide by 1.175
To identify problems like this, look for words which suggest going back in time, like:
'What was the original cost?'
'How much was the item to start with?'
'How much did he/she buy it for?'

TEST YOURSELF

1 Find the interest rate if £60 saved for 1 year becomes: **a** £64.59 **b** £64.98

2 Jenny invests £840 at 6% compound interest for 4 years. Find:
 a the total amount after 8 years
 b the total compound interest.

3 A dealer sells a washing machine for £372. He makes 25% profit.
What did the machine cost the dealer?

4 Alex sells his bike for £64. He makes a 24% loss. How much did the bike cost him originally?

Indices

☐ Squares and square roots

The square numbers are: 1 4 9 16 25…
They come from   1×1 2×2 3×3 4×4 5×5…
which are also   1²   2²   3²   4²   5²

A **square** is the special name for a **power of 2**.

To find a square root you have to undo a square.
So because 4 × 4 = 16 the square root of 16 is 4.

You can think of it like this:

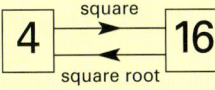

See also > **Types of number** page 6

☐ Cubes and cube roots

The cube numbers are: 1 8 27 64 125…
They come from   1×1×1 2×2×2 3×3×3 4×4×4 5×5×5…
which are also   1³   2³   3³   4³   5³

A **cube** is the special name for a **power of 3**.

To find a cube root you have to undo a cube.
So because 3 × 3 × 3 = 27 the cube root of 27 is 3.

You can think of it like this:

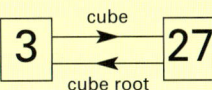

☐ Powers

It is easier to write 2 + 2 + 2 + 2 as 4 × 2.
You can write 2 × 2 × 2 × 2 more easily as 2^4.
This means 2 to the power of 4 and it has the value 16.

Example
Work out $2^5 \times 5^2$

2^5 means five 2s multiplied by each other.

$2^5 \times 5^2$ = 2 × 2×2 × 2×2 × 5×5
       = 2 × 4 × 4 × 25
       = 100 × 8   = 800

☐ Using a power key on a calculator

You can use the y^x key or x^y key to work out any power.

To find 2^6 key in

to get 64.

Notes

The square numbers are
1 4 9 16 25…

You can find them on a calculator using the x^2 key.

You do the opposite of squaring to find a square root.

You can use the √ key on your calculator to find a square root.

Use the x^y key or the y^x key on your calculator to find a cube.

To do 4^3, key in 4 x^y 3 = to get 64.

A cube root is shown as $\sqrt[3]{}$

Use the $x^{1/y}$ key or the $\sqrt[x]{}$ key on your calculator to find a cube root.

To do $\sqrt[3]{64}$, key in $\sqrt[x]{}$ 6 4 3 to get 4.

You have four 2s *added* together.
You have four 2s *multiplied* together.

Without a calculator   2 × 2 × 2 × 2
you can work it out   =   4 × 2 × 2
like this.   =   8 × 2
                      =   16

A common mistake is to write 3^4 as 12. This is because you might think it means 4 lots of 3.

This helps to only multiply two numbers at a time. As soon as you get 3 × 3 = 9 you will realise that 3^4 cannot be 12.

In x^n the number x is called the base.
In x^n the number n is called the index or power. The plural of index is indices.
Here 2 is the base and 6 is the index.

☐ Rules of indices

Look at $4^3 \times 4^2$. This is $4 \times 4 \times 4 \times 4 \times 4 = 4^5$

You can get this answer if you add the indices $4^{3+2} = 4^5$

You can show this rule with letters. $a^m \times a^n = a^{m+n}$

Look at $4^3 \div 4^2$. This is $\dfrac{4 \times 4 \times 4}{4 \times 4} = 4^1$ or $4^{3-2} = 4^1$

Using letters this rule is $a^m \div a^n = a^{m-n}$

Look at $(4^3)^2$. This is $4^3 \times 4^3 = 4^{3+3} = 4^6$

This is the same as $4^{3 \times 2} = 4^6$

Here is the rule using letters. $(a^m)^n = a^{m \times n}$

Notes
You can only do this if the base numbers are the same. So $2^4 \times 3^2$ cannot be done.
$2^4 \times 3^2 = 16 \times 9 = 144$
144 is not 5^6 or 6^6 or 2^6 or 3^6!

Examples

Work out: **a** $2^4 \times 2^3$ **b** $5^6 \div 5^2$ **c** $(3^2)^4$

a Using $a^m \times a^n = a^{m+n}$, $2^4 \times 2^3 = 2^{4+3} = 2^7$

b Using $a^m \div a^n = a^{m-n}$, $5^6 \div 5^2 = 5^{6-2} = 5^4$

c Using $(a^m)^n = a^{m \times n}$, $(3^2)^4 = 3^{2 \times 4} = 3^8$

☐ Zero and negative powers

For any number a, $a^0 = 1$ and $a^{-1} = \dfrac{1}{a}$

$\dfrac{1}{a}$ is called the **reciprocal** of a,

$\dfrac{b}{a}$ is the **reciprocal** of $\dfrac{a}{b}$

$\dfrac{1}{2}$ is called the reciprocal of 2.

$\dfrac{5}{7}$ is called the reciprocal of $\dfrac{7}{5}$.

Examples

Work out: **a** 7^0 **b** 5^{-1} **c** $(1\tfrac{1}{3})^{-1}$

a $7^0 = 1$ **b** $5^{-1} = \tfrac{1}{5}$ **c** $(1\tfrac{1}{3})^{-1} = (\tfrac{4}{3})^{-1} = \tfrac{3}{4}$

You will notice that you need to make a mixed number like $1\tfrac{1}{3}$ improper before trying to find its reciprocal.

☐ Standard form – big numbers

A number in standard form has two parts:
a number from 1 up to 9.9... multiplied by 10 to a power.

To write a number like 240 000 in standard form:

* put an arrow after the first digit.
  This is where the new
  decimal point goes.   2↓4 0 0 0 0   So the number will be $2.4 \times 10^?$

* count the other digits along to the real
  decimal point. This is the power of 10.   2 4 0 0 0 0 1 2 3 4 5

So the number is 2.4×10^5 in standard form.

To work out the value of a number in standard form you use the same sort of process. Put an arrow after the first digit, then count the power of 10.

So $4.5 \times 10^9 = 4\,5\,0\,0\,0\,0\,0\,0\,0\,0 = 4\,500\,000\,000$

Or you can use the 'moving arrow' method. Put the new decimal point after the first digit.

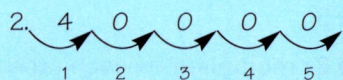

When you move it back to where it should go, it has moved 5 places.

Chapter 22 pages 63–65

Or use the arrow method and add noughts to fill the gaps.

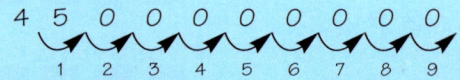

☐ Standard form – small numbers

You can use the same process as with big numbers to put numbers in and out of standard form. The only difference is that numbers less than 1 have **negative** powers.

Examples

a Write 0.000 000 056 09 in standard form.

0.000 000 056 09 = 5.609×10^{-8}
(count: 8 7 6 5 4 3 2 1)

b Work out the value of 6.3877×10^{-6}

0.000 006 387 7 = 0.000 006 387 7
(count: 6 5 4 3 2 1)

☐ Standard form on calculator displays

Very large numbers get changed on calculator displays.
Some new calculators display 2.3×10^9 like this $2.3^{\times 10^{09}}$
Others still display 2.3×10^9 like this 2.3^{09}

☐ Using the EXP or EE key on a calculator

To enter 4.62×10^7 key in [4] [.] [6] [2] [EXP] [7]
To enter 2.9×10^5 key in [2] [.] [9] [EXP] [5]

Example

Work out: $\dfrac{(4 \times 10^8) \times (7.1 \times 10^9)}{(9 \times 10^7) \div (4.5 \times 10^{-5})}$ Give your answer in standard form.

Top line:
Key in [4] [EXP] [8] [×] [7] [.] [1] [EXP] [9] [=] 2.84×10^{18}

Bottom line:
Key in [9] [EXP] [7] [÷] [4] [.] [5] [EXP] [5] [±] [=] 2×10^{12}

Finally [2] [.] [8] [4] [EXP] [1] [7] [÷] [2] [EXP] [1] [2] [=] 1.42×10^5

Notes

Notice that you always count **from** the arrow.

Calculators use notation close to standard form.

You need to be sure you can write down these displays in standard form. You must make sure you put the '× 10' part in or write the number the right size.

Some calculators have an [EE] key or an [Exp] key instead of an [EXP] key. If yours has, use it in exactly the same way as shown for the [EXP] key.

Chapter 22 pages 65–66

You need to use BODMAS here. The top and bottom of this expression will have brackets around them because of the large divide line.

$\dfrac{[(4 \times 10^8) \times (7.1 \times 10^9)]}{[(9 \times 10^7) \div (4.5 \times 10^{-5})]}$

TEST YOURSELF

1 Work these out. Show all your working.
   a 6^2 **b** 5^3 **c** $\sqrt{289}$
   d $3\sqrt{64}$ **e** $5^4 \times 3^2$ **f** $5^4 \times 5^2$
   g $(5^4)^2$ **h** 7^0 **i** 4^{-2}

2 Write these numbers in standard form.
   a 22 000 **b** 0.046
   c 39 200 000 000 **d** 0.000 059 24
   e 700 million **f** $2\frac{3}{4}$ million

3 Write these calculator displays in standard form.
   a $5^{\times 10^{08}}$ **b** 1.48^{22} **c** $6.093^{\times 10^{-12}}$

4 Use a calculator to work these out. Give your answer in standard form.
   a $(2 \times 10^8)^2$ **b** $\dfrac{(1.08 \times 10^6) \div (3 \times 10^{-10})}{(4.5 \times 10^8) \times (4 \times 10^{-2})}$

Practice questions

1 a Write **each** of the following numbers in standard form.

    i 734 800 000

    ii 0.000 57   (2)

  b Find, in standard form, the value of **each** of the following.

    i $(3.42 \times 10^4) \times (5.91 \times 10^{-11})$

    ii $\dfrac{4.69 \times 10^{-6}}{7.45 \times 10^4}$ (4)

WJEC, 1999, Paper 0184/5

2 a Harold invests £850 at 8% p.a. simple interest. Calculate the total amount of money he has at the end of three years. (3)

  b Katherine invests £600 in a simple interest account. At the end of two years her investment has become £684. What is the annual percentage rate of simple interest? (2)

WJEC, 1999, Paper D184/5

3 a Express the number $\tfrac{3}{5}$ as a percentage. (1)

  b List the following in order of size, starting with the smallest.

    $\tfrac{2}{3}$, 0.7, 0.67, 66%. (2)

  c Calculate the exact value of

    i $\tfrac{1}{2} + \tfrac{2}{3}$, (1)

    ii $\tfrac{4}{5}$ of $2\tfrac{1}{2}$, (1)

    iii $5 \div \tfrac{2}{3}$. (1)

OCR, 1999, Paper 1662/3

4 In this question you must **NOT** use a calculator.
You must show **ALL** your working.

Tom buys 67 cameras at £312 each.

  a Work out the total cost. (3)

  b Write down two numbers you could use to get an approximate answer to your calculation. (2)

Edexcel, 1999, Paper 3

2 Algebra

- [ ] **Patterns in numbers**
- [ ] **Use of algebra**
- [ ] **Graphs of straight lines**
- [ ] **Practical graphs**
- [ ] **Solving equations**
- [ ] **Curved graphs**
- [ ] **Inequalities**

Practice questions

Patterns in numbers

☐ Number sequences

A **number sequence** is a list of numbers that follows a rule.
Each number in the sequence is called a **term**.
You can write a formula for a number sequence.
The multiples of 4 form a sequence   4   8   12   16 …
The formula for this sequence is $m = 4n$ where n is the term number.
You can work out any term using this formula.
To find the tenth term you substitute 10 for n.
The tenth term is $10 \times 4 = 40$.

Notes

The multiples of 2 have the formula $m = 2n$
The multiples of 3 have the formula $m = 3n$
The multiples of 5 have the formula $m = 5n$
and so on…

☐ Finding a formula with two parts

These patterns are made up of dots.

The number of dots in the pattern can be written as a number sequence. To find a formula for the sequence use d for the number of dots.
The number sequence is   4   7   10   13
The pattern goes up in threes. It is related to $m = 3n$.
Write the terms of $m = 3n$ underneath the sequence.

```
         4    7    10    13
                              ↑  + 1
3n       3    6    9    12
```

You have to add 1 to get the sequence.
The formula is $d = 3n + 1$
You can use the formula to find the number of dots in the 50th pattern.
$d = 3 \times 50 + 1 = 151$
There are 151 dots in the 50th pattern.
You can also use this formula to find the number of the pattern that has 85 dots.
85   $= 3n + 1$
84   $= 3n$
so $n = 28$.
The 28th pattern has 85 dots.

Find the difference between terms.
The rule is 'add 3' but the sequence is not the multiples of 3. The multiples of 3 start with 3.

Check that the formula works by using it to find a term you already know.
The fourth term = $3 \times 4 + 1 = 13$

Chapter 4 pages 86–94

Substitute 85 for d.
Subtract 1 from each side.
Divide by three.

TEST YOURSELF

1 **a** Write down the first six multiples of 8.
   b Write down the formula for the sequence.
   c Use your formula to find the 100th term.

2 **a** Find the rule for this number sequence:
       55   50   45   40   35   …
   b Find the tenth term.
   c Which term has the value −5?

3 These patterns are made with matchsticks.

   a Draw the next pattern.
   b Write down the number of matchsticks as a number sequence.
   c Work out the formula for the number of matchsticks.

Number sequences with an n^2 term

You need to find the formula for the following number sequence:

5 18 37 62 93

5		18		37		62		93
	13		19		25		31	
		6		6		6		

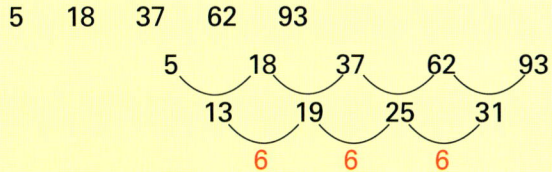

If the **second differences** are the same, the formula for the nth term contains n^2. The coefficient of n^2 is half the second difference.
The second difference is 6, so the coefficient of n^2 is 3.
The first part of the formula is $3n^2$.

By writing a table you can find the rest of the formula.

Term number	1	2	3	4	5
Sequence	5	18	37	62	93
	↑+2	↑+6	↑+10	↑+14	↑+18
Value of $3n^2$	3	12	27	48	75

Now look for what you need to add to get the sequence. 2 6 10 14 18

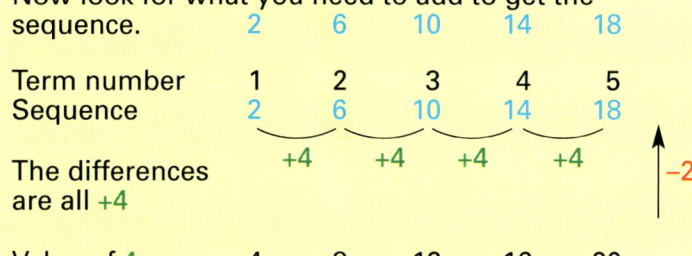

Term number	1	2	3	4	5	
Sequence	2	6	10	14	18	
The differences are all +4	+4	+4	+4	+4		↑ −2
Value of $4n$	4	8	12	16	20	

The formula for the second part is $4n - 2$.
You can now put the two parts of the formula together.
The formula for the nth term of the sequence is:

$$3n^2 + 4n - 2$$

Check the formula by working out the fifth term.

When $n = 5$, $3n^2 + 4n - 2 = 75 + 20 - 2 = 93$ ✔

Notes

Look at the differences between the terms

These differences are not the same.
Look at the differences between these numbers.
These are called the second differences.

The coefficient of n^2 is the number in front of n^2.

n^2 is	1,	4,	9,	16,	25,	…
$2n^2$ is	2,	8,	18,	32,	50,	…
$3n^2$ is	3,	12,	27,	48,	75,	…

Subtract the sequence from the value of $3n^2$, to find the number you need to add to give the sequence.

Find the rest of the sequence as you did before.

Always check your formula by working out the value of a term you already know.

Chapter 24 pages 113–117

TEST YOURSELF

1 For the following sequences:

(1) find the formula for the nth term
(2) check your formula by working out the fifth term.

a	4	9	16	25	36
b	2	8	16	26	38
c	7	14	25	40	59
d	9	23	45	75	113

2 The formula for a sequence is $3n^2 + 4n - 1$.

a Find the first four terms.
b Find the 10th term.

3 The formula for a sequence is $5n^2 - 2n + 3$.

a Find the first four terms.
b Find the tenth term.

Use of algebra

☐ Collecting terms

In algebra you can **collect terms** together as long as they are the same type.

$a + a + a + a + a + a = 6a$

$b + b + b + b + c + c + c = 4b + 3c$

$d^2 + 6d^2 - 2d^2 + 3d = 5d^2 + 3d$

☐ Multiplying terms

When you multiply two letters together you can miss out the multiplication sign.

When you are multiplying numbers and letters the numbers always come before the letters.

If the letters are the same you should write them as powers.

☐ Expanding a bracket

All the terms inside a bracket must be multiplied by the number on the outside.

You must look at the signs carefully and remember the rules about multiplying positive and negative numbers.

Examples

$5(2a - 3) = 5 \times 2a + 5 \times (-3)$
$\qquad\quad = 10a - 15$

$-4(3r^2 - 5r) = -4 \times 3r^2 + (-4) \times (-5r)$
$\qquad\qquad\quad = -12r^2 + 20r$

$3m(m + 6n) = 3m \times m + 3m \times 6n$
$\qquad\qquad\quad = 3m^2 + 18mn$

Notes

You cannot add bs and cs together.

Terms in d^2 and d cannot be added together.

Chapter 6 pages 120

$k \times l = kl$

$2p \times 3q = 6pq$

$3x \times 4x = 12x^2$

Chapter 15 pages 322–323

×/÷	+	−
+	+	−
−	−	+

Chapter 27 pages 166–167

TEST YOURSELF

1 Simplify these by collecting terms.
   a $3h + 4h + 2h - 5h$
   b $6a + 4b - 2a + 3b$
   c $5xy + 7xy - xy$
   d $3x^2 + x^2$

2 Simplify these.
   a $6t \times 7t$
   b $4f \times 3f \times 5g$

3 Multiply out these brackets.
   a $3(w + 2)$
   b $-4(c^2 + 6)$
   c $5(a^2 - 2a + 9)$
   d $k(k + 8)$
   e $m(2n - m)$

28

☐ Multiplying out two brackets

When you multiply out two brackets you must remember to multiply all the terms in the second bracket by all the terms in the first bracket.

Don't forget to collect the terms together.

$(x + 2)(x - 6)$
$= x^2 - 6x + 2x - 12$
$= x^2 - 4x - 12$

☐ Factorising

Factorising is the opposite of multiplying out brackets. First you must look for a common factor in the numbers.
You can also take letters outside the brackets as common factors.
$6x + 15y = 3(2x + 5y)$
$ab - bc = b(a - c)$
$g^2 - g^3 = g^2(1 - g)$

In this expression $x^2 + 6x + 8$
6 is the coefficient of x and 8 is the constant.

$x^2 + 6x + 8$ will factorise into two brackets.
The brackets will be $(x + ...)(x + ...)$

The numbers at the end of the brackets must add to give 6, the coefficient of x, and multiply to give 8, the constant.
These numbers must be 2 and 4.
So, $x^2 + 6x + 8 = (x + 2)(x + 4)$

It is helpful to look at the signs in the expression you are factorising.

$x^2 + 6x + 8$
$= (x + 2)(x + 4)$ — The number at the end is +8. The numbers must be the same sign to give a + when they are multiplied together. They must both be + to add to give +6. They are 2 and 4.

$x^2 - 5x + 4$
$= (x - 1)(x - 4)$ — The number at the end is +4. The numbers must be the same sign to give a + when they are multiplied together. They must both be − to add to give −5. They are −1 and −4.

$x^2 + 2x - 15$
$= (x - 3)(x + 5)$ — The number at the end is −15. The numbers must have different signs to give a − when they are multiplied together. The + number must be larger because they add to give a + total of +2. They are 5 and −3.

Notes

Remember **FOIL** or the face.

Multiply the two **F**irst terms together.
Multiply the two **O**utside terms together.
Multiply the two **I**nside terms together.
Multiply the two **L**ast terms together.

Chapter 15 pages 325–326

Chapter 27 pages 169–171

When you have found a number that divides into both the numbers in the expression, check that you have found the largest factor.

It is very important that you don't forget the 1 inside this bracket.

Always check your factorising by multiplying out the bracket. You must get back to the expression you started with.

A quadratic expression has a term in x^2. It must not have any higher power of x, or a term such as $\frac{1}{x}$.

You can write the brackets either way round.

This process is known as **factorising a quadratic**.

Chapter 27 pages 172–174

29

☐ Factorising the difference of two squares

A quadratic expression which is of the form $x^2 - a^2$ is known as the **difference of two squares**.

To factorise $x^2 - 25$, think of the expression as $x^2 + 0x - 25$.
The numbers in the two brackets must add to give 0 and multiply to give -25.

The numbers must be $+5$ and -5.
$x^2 - 25 = (x + 5)(x - 5)$

The general rule is $x^2 - a^2 = (x + a)(x - a)$

Notes

The word difference means subtract.

Chapter 27 page 174

☐ Changing the subject

The **subject of a formula** is the letter that is written on its own, usually on the left-hand side.

To change the subject of a formula you must use the same methods as when solving an equation.

Example 1
Make b the subject of the formula $a = 5b + c$

$$a - c = 5b$$
$$5b = a - c$$
$$b = \frac{a - c}{5}$$

Subtract c from both sides to leave the $5b$ on its own.
Write the formula the other way round.
Divide by 5 on both sides to leave b on its own.

Example 2
Make f the subject of the formula $2d = \frac{4e - 7f}{3}$

$$6d = 4e - 7f$$
$$6d + 7f = 4e$$
$$7f = 4e - 6d$$
$$f = \frac{4e - 6d}{7}$$

Multiply by 3.
Add $7f$ to both sides.
Subtract $6d$ from both sides.

Divide by 7 to leave f.

Example 3
Make m the subject of the formula $k = \sqrt{3m - 2l}$
$$k^2 = m - 2l$$
$$k^2 + 2l = m$$
$$m = k^2 + 2l$$

To remove the square root, square each side.
Add $2l$ to both sides.

Chapter 20 pages 36–38

TEST YOURSELF

1 Multiply out the brackets:
 a $(2x - 3)(3x + 4)$
 b $(5y - 6)(y - 2)$
 c $(xy + 4)(2xy + 7)$

2 Factorise the following:
 a $x^2 + 5x + 6$
 b $x^2 + 2x - 8$
 c $x^2 - 6x + 5$

3 Factorise:
 a $x^2 - 9$
 b $r^2 - 169$
 c $a^2 - b^2$

4 Change the subject to x in each of the following:
 a $3y = 2z + 4x$
 b $t = \frac{x - s}{5}$
 c $s = \sqrt{4x + t}$

Graphs of straight lines

☐ Co-ordinates and equations of horizontal and vertical lines

Co-ordinates are used to describe the location of points and are written in the form (x, y).
The first number is the x co-ordinate. It gives the horizontal distance from the origin.
The second number is the y co-ordinate. It gives the vertical distance from the origin.

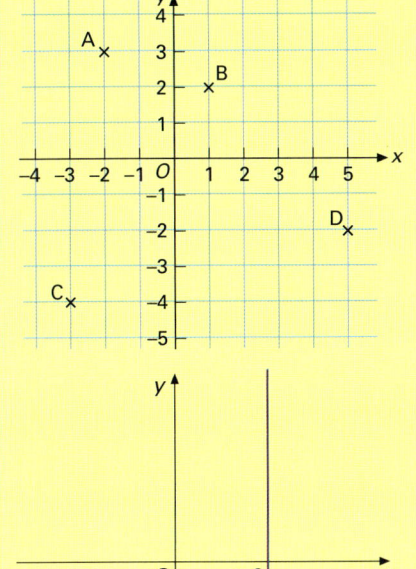

A is the point $(-2, 3)$,
B is $(1, 2)$,
C is $(-3, -4)$,
D is $(5, -2)$.

The x co-ordinate of all the points on the blue line is 2.
The equation of this line is $x = 2$

The y co-ordinate of all the points on the red line is -3.
The equation of this line is $y = -3$

Notes

The horizontal value is always given first.

The equation of all vertical lines is written as
$$x = a$$
where a is the point where the line crosses the x axis.

The equation of all horizontal lines is written as
$$y = b$$
where b is the point where the line crosses the y axis.

Chapter 1 pages 2–6

☐ Gradients

The **gradient** of a line is a measure of the slope of the line, or how steep the line is.
To find the gradient of a line you need to take two points on the line which are not too close together.

Gradient = $\dfrac{\text{vertical change}}{\text{horizontal change}}$

$= \dfrac{7}{4}$

The gradient of the line is $\dfrac{7}{4}$.

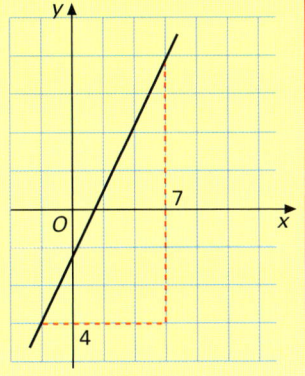

The gradient of a horizontal line is zero.

The vertical change is the difference between the y co-ordinates of the two points chosen.

The horizontal change is the difference between the x co-ordinates of the two points chosen.

Lines sloping from bottom left to top right have a positive gradient.

31

This line slopes the opposite way.
It has a negative gradient.

Gradient = $\dfrac{\text{vertical change}}{\text{horizontal change}}$

$= \dfrac{-4}{2}$

$= -2$

The gradient of this line is −2.

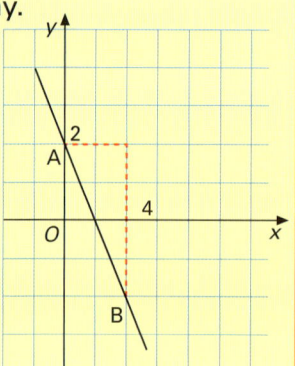

The vertical change from A to B is negative, which gives a negative gradient.

Lines sloping from top left to bottom right have a negative gradient.

☐ y = mx + c

The equation of any straight line can be written as
$y = mx + c$

The line has gradient m and cuts the y axis at c.

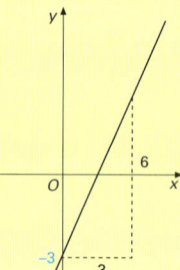

The equation of this line is

$y = 2x - 3$

Chapter 8 pages 162–169

The equation of a straight line is called a linear equation.

The gradient of the line is 2.
The line cuts the y axis at −3.

☐ Parallel lines

Lines that have the same gradient are **parallel lines**.

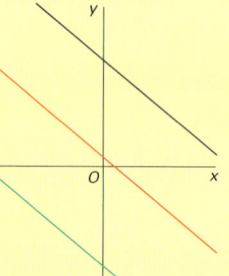

Each of these lines has the same gradient, although they cut the y axis at different points.

These three lines are parallel.

You can spot parallel lines without drawing them.
These lines are parallel:
$y = 2x - 3$, $y = 4 + 2x$ $y = 2x + 16$
All of these equations has + 2x in them.

The gradient of a straight line is given by the co-efficient of x.
The co-efficient of x is 2 in each of these equations. So the gradient of these parallel lines is 2.

Chapter 8 pages 170–171

☐ Using straight line graphs to solve problems

Sometimes you can use a straight line graph to help solve a problem.

Example

A tank is full of water that is then allowed to flow out at a steady speed. The following graph shows how the volume in the tank changes. The formula for the volume is $v = a - bt$, where t is the time in minutes.

32

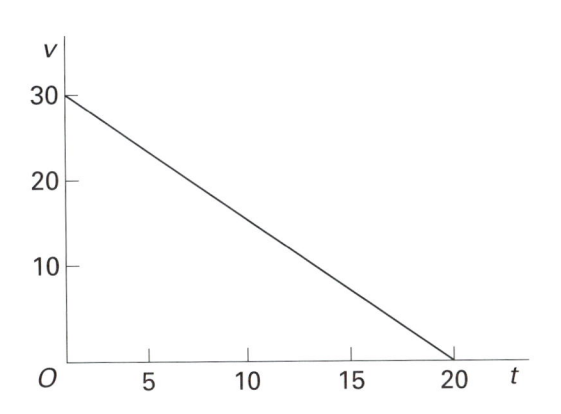

The value of *a* is the volume of water in the tank initially. You can see from the graph that $a = 30$ litres.
b is the rate at which the water flows out of the tank in litres per minute. You can find the value of *b* by calculating the gradient of the line.
The gradient is -1.5.
The equation of the line is $v = 30 - 1.5t$.

☐ Drawing graphs of *ax + by = c*

Example
Draw the graph of the equation $3x + 4y = 12$

When $x = 0$; $(3 \times 0) + 4y = 12$
so $\qquad\qquad\qquad 4y = 12$
so $\qquad\qquad\qquad\;\; y = 3$
(0, 3) is on the line.

When $y = 0$; $3x + (4 \times 0) = 12$
so $\qquad\qquad\qquad 3x = 12$
so $\qquad\qquad\qquad\;\; x = 4$
(4, 0) is on the line.

The line goes through the points (0, 3) and (4, 0).

Now it can be drawn.

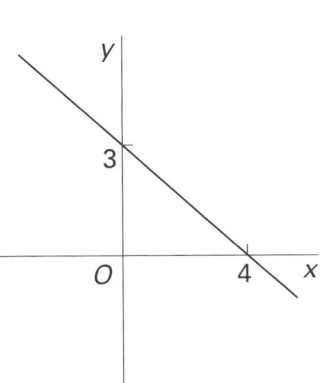

Notes

If the tank is emptying at a **steady** speed then the graph will be a straight line. The gradient is constant.

The gradient is negative because the water is flowing out of the tank. In other words the volume is decreasing.

$y = mx + c$ is one version of the equation of a straight line.
$ax + by = c$ is another version.

a, *b*, and *c* are numbers, or constants.

An equation with x^2 or $\frac{1}{x}$ is not linear.

The line cuts the *y* axis when $x = 0$.
The line cuts the *x* axis when $y = 0$.

Chapter 8 pages 175–179

TEST YOURSELF

1 Find the gradient of the line passing through the points:
  a (3, 4) and (8, 14)
  b (−1, −4) and (2, 2)
  c (0, 6) and (1, 7)

2 Write down the gradient of each of these lines.
  a $y = 2x - 3$
  b $y = -x + 2$
  c $y = 5 - 3x$

3 Write down where each of the lines in question **2** cuts the *y* axis.

4 Which of these points lie on the line $y = 3x - 2$?
  a (1, 1)   **b** (−1, −5)   **c** (2, 3)

5 Which of these equations is linear?
  a $y = 4x - 5$
  b $y = x^2 + 1$
  c $2y = 1.4x + 7$

6 Draw the graph of these lines:
  a $2x - 3y = 6$
  b $3x - y = 12$
  c $4x + 5y = 20$

Practical graphs

☐ Time, distance and speed

Problems involving time, distance and speed can be solved easily if you learn the formulas you need.

This triangle can help you remember these formulas.

Cover up the letter you want and you will see the formula.

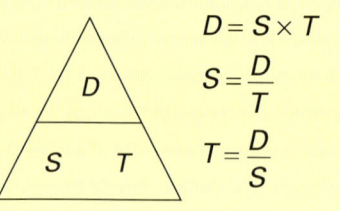

$D = S \times T$

$S = \dfrac{D}{T}$

$T = \dfrac{D}{S}$

☐ Travel graphs

Travel graphs are used to show distance and time. They show you the distance that something has moved over a period of time.

You can work out speeds by finding the gradient of the graph.

This graph shows John's journey from Northampton to Wolverhampton.

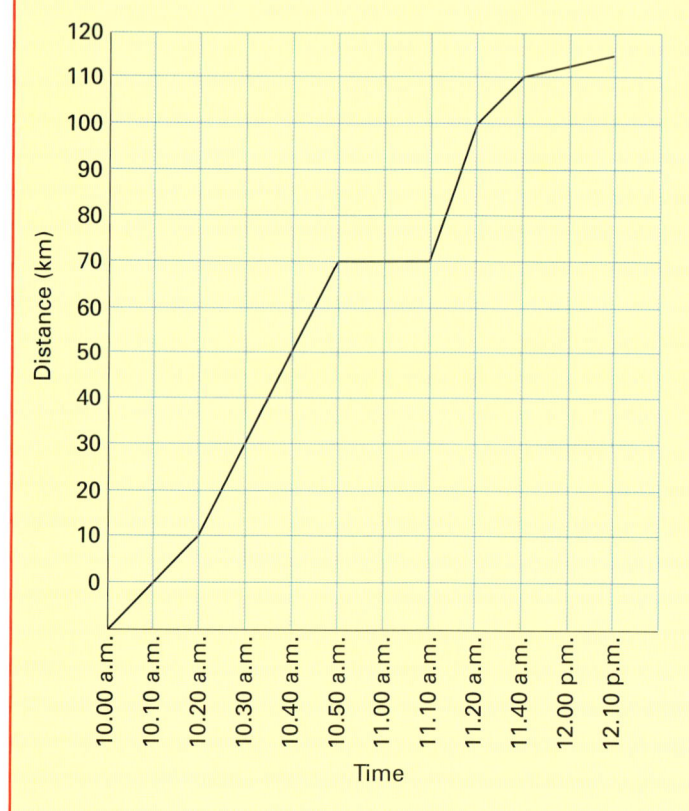

The total distance is 115 km and the total time is 2 h 10 min, which equals $2\tfrac{1}{6}$ hours.

$= 2.1\dot{6}$ hours

So the average speed $= \dfrac{115}{2.1\dot{6}}$

$= 53.1$ km/h (1 dp)

Notes

When time is given in hours remember that you must convert any minutes into a decimal, or fraction, of an hour.
E.g. 2 hours 45 minutes must be written as 2.75 hours.

Think carefully about the units you give in your answers.
E.g. km for distance, hours for time and km/h for speed.

Chapter 13 pages 278–281

Time always goes on the horizontal axis and distance goes on the vertical axis.

The steeper the slope the faster John is travelling.

Between 10.50 a.m. and 11.10 a.m. the line is horizontal. This tells you that John is not moving i.e. he has stopped for 20 minutes. His speed here is zero.

The average speed for the whole journey can be calculated as

Average speed $= \dfrac{\text{total distance}}{\text{total time}}$

Chapter 13 pages 282–285

34

☐ Step graphs

When you draw graphs, usually you plot some points then join them with lines. You must think carefully what these lines are showing. Sometimes you may have gaps between the lines.

This **step graph** shows the cost of sending a first class letter.

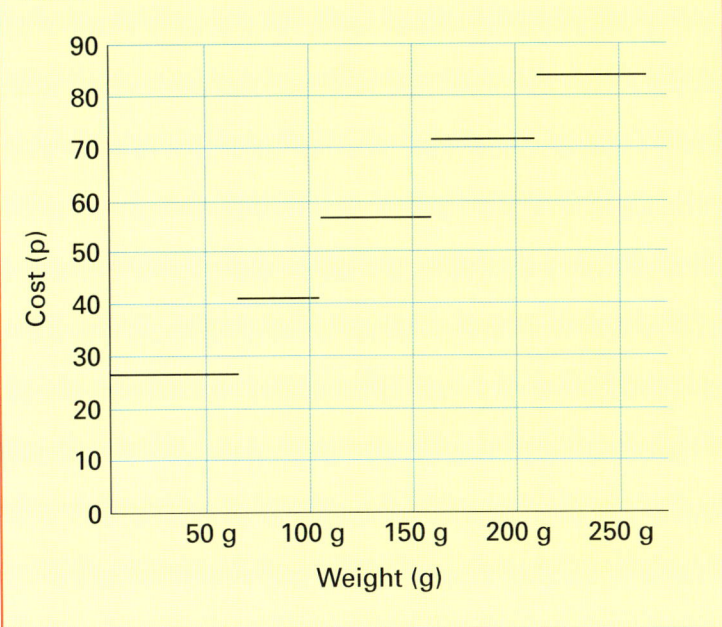

Notes

All letters up to 60 g cost 27p.
All letters weighing between 60 g and 100 g cost 4p.
Letters weighing up to 150 g cost 57p, and so on.

The lines cannot be joined together.

Chapter 13 pages 287–288

☐ Conversion graphs

A **conversion graph** is a graph that enables you to change from one unit to another. For example you could change one currency to another, or change from pounds to kilograms.

A conversion graph is always a straight line graph.

This graph allows you to convert pounds into kilograms.

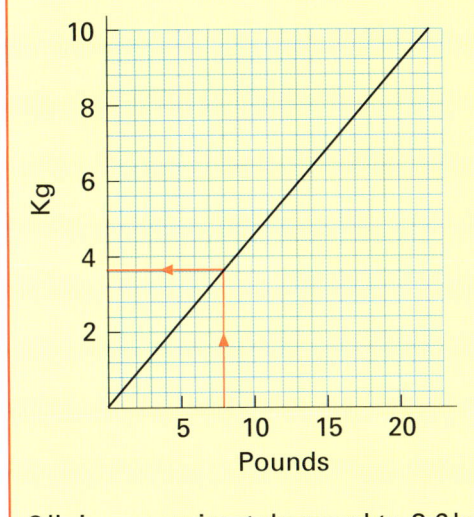

8 lb is approximately equal to 3.6 kg.

To convert 8 lb into kg you must draw a line from 8 lb up to the line, then go across and read off the value on the vertical axis. This is shown by the red lines.

Chapter 13 pages 289–290

Graph sketching

A **sketch graph** does not have an accurate scale on its axes. It is drawn to show a pattern or trend. It is not used to give accurate readings.

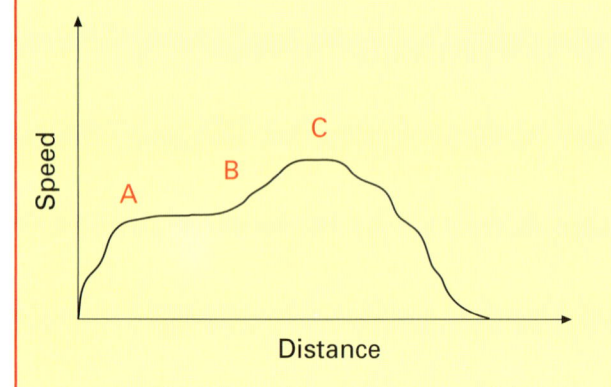

[Graph: Speed vs Distance showing points A, B, C]

This graph shows Sarah's journey to school by bicycle.
She speeds up when she leaves home then cycles at a steady speed between A and B.
She cycles faster between B and C and slows down as she approaches school.

Notes

Although there is no scale on the axes they should always be labelled.

Chapter 13 pages 291–297

TEST YOURSELF

1. A car travels a distance of 245 km at an average speed of 55 km per hour. How long does the journey take?

2. James walks at a speed of 4 km/h for 25 minutes. He then waits 35 minutes for a bus. He travels on the bus for an hour at a speed of 40 km/h. Draw a travel graph to show his journey.

   Work out the average speed for the journey.

3. This table shows the cost of posting second class mail.

Weight up to...	60 g	100 g	150 g	200 g	250 g
Cost	19p	33p	44p	54p	66p

   Draw a graph to show these costs.

4. £1 is equivalent to 1.6 Euros. Draw a conversion graph to change from £ to €.

   Draw axes from £0 to £20 and €0 to €40.

   a Use your graph to convert £15 to Euros.
   b Use the graph to convert €20 to £.

5. Shane cycles to school. The first part of his journey is along a level road. He slows down as he cycles uphill. He rests for a few minutes before cycling downhill quickly. He slows down as he reaches the school gate. Using distance and speed axes, sketch a graph of his journey from the description given.

Solving equations

☐ Solving linear equations

> **Linear equations** do not contain term like x^2, x^3 or $\frac{1}{x}$. They only have x terms and numbers.
>
> When you solve an equation you are working out the value of the letter.

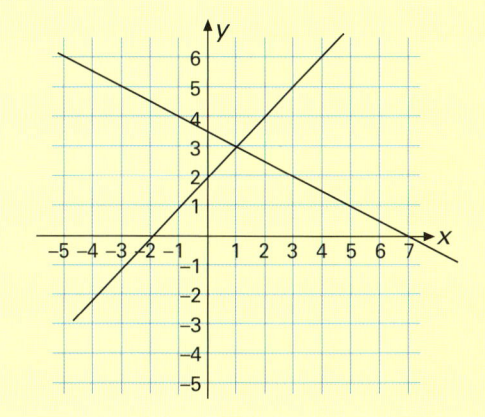

Notes

Remember to get the letter onto one side of the equation.

Example 1

$$2x + 3 = 15$$
$$2x + 3 - 3 = 15 - 3$$
$$2x = 12$$
$$\frac{2x}{2} = \frac{12}{2}$$
$$x = 6$$

Subtract 3 from both sides.

Divide both sides by 2.

Example 2

$$6x - 4 = 3x + 8$$
$$6x - 3x - 4 = 3x - 3x + 8$$
$$3x - 4 = 8$$
$$3x - 4 + 4 = 8 + 4$$
$$3x = 12$$
$$x = 4$$

Subtracting 3x from both sides so that x is only on one side of the equation.
Add 4 to both sides.

Divide both sides by 3.

Example 3

$$5(3x - 1) = 3(x + 15)$$
$$15x - 5 = 3x + 45$$
$$12x - 5 = 45$$
$$12x = 50$$
$$x = 4\tfrac{1}{6}$$

First multiply out the brackets, then solve as usual.

Chapter 6 pages 127–131

☐ Simultaneous equations

> When you solve two equations at the same time you are solving **simultaneous equations**.
> You can solve simultaneous equations by drawing graphs.
>
> If you want to solve the equations $y = x + 2$ and $x + 2y = 7$, you must first draw these straight lines and find the co-ordinates of the point where the lines cross.

The lines cross at the point (1, 3).
You should check that this solution works in both equations.

Chapter 20 pages 26–29

37

You can also solve simultaneous equations by using algebraic methods.

You need to eliminate one of the variables (usually x or y).

Look to see if the terms have the same coefficient. If the signs are the **s**ame you can eliminate that letter by **s**ubtracting. If the signs are different you should add the equations to eliminate the letter.

Notes

Remember that **s**ame signs should be **s**ubtracted.

Examples

1 Solve simultaneously:
$$x + y = 15$$
$$3x - y = 9$$

The coefficients of y are 1.
The signs of y are different so you add the equations.
This gives
$$4x = 24$$
$$x = 6$$
$$x + y = 15$$
$$\text{So } 6 + y = 15$$
$$y = 9$$

The answer is $x = 6$, $y = 9$.

Always check your answer by substituting back into both equations.

2 Solve simultaneously:
$$4x + 2y = 17$$
$$3x + 2y = 14$$

The coefficients of y are 2.
The signs of y are the same so you subtract the equations.
$$x = 3$$

To find y, put $x = 3$ into the first equation.
$$4 \times 3 + 2y = 17$$
$$12 + 2y = 17$$
$$2y = 5$$
$$y = 2\tfrac{1}{2}$$

The answer is $x = 3$, $y = 2\tfrac{1}{2}$.

Check by substituting back into both equations.

If the terms do not have the same coefficients, you need to multiply one (or both) of the equations by a number before you can add or subtract.

Example

Solve this pair of simultaneous equations.
$$3a + 4b = 41$$
$$4a - 5b = 3$$

Number the equations.
(1) $3a + 4b = 41$
(2) $4a - 5b = 3$

Multiply (1) by 5.   (1) × 5 $15a + 20b = 205$
Multiply (2) by 4.   (2) × 4 $16a - 20b = 12$
Add to eliminate b. $31a = 217$
                                $a = 7$

Put $a = 7$ into equation (1)

Use equation (1) to find b. $21 + 4b = 41$
                                $4b = 20$
                                $b = 5$

Chapter 20 pages 30–35

Remember to check the answer in both equations.

The answer is $a = 7$, $b = 5$.

Solving quadratic equations

If you can factorise a quadratic expression, you can solve quadratic equations. When you solve a quadratic equation you are finding where the graph cuts the x axis.

Notes

Factorise the quadratic. You must have an expression equal to zero before trying to factorise.

Example
Solve the equation $x^2 - x - 6 = 0$

Factorising $(x - 3)(x + 2) = 0$
so $(x - 3) = 0$ or $(x + 2) = 0$
so $x = 3$ or $x = -2$

If two brackets are multiplied together and give the answer zero, then at least one of the brackets must equal zero. Quadratic equations always have two solutions.

The graph of $y = x^2 - x - 6$ looks like this.

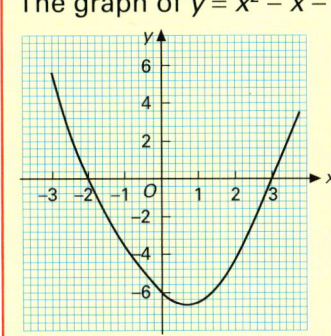

The values for x you have worked out are the co-ordinates of the points where the curve cuts the x axis.

When $x = 0$, $y = -6$ so the curve passes through $(0, -6)$ too.

The points where the quadratic curve cuts the x axis are often referred to as the roots of the equation.

Quadratic graphs are always symmetrical.

Chapter 27 pages 175–179

Trial and improvement

Sometimes you need to solve an equation that does not factorise, or cannot be solved using a formula. You can use the method of **trial and improvement** to find a solution to this type of equation.

Example
Solve the equation $x^3 + x = 172$. Give the answer to 1 decimal place.

Value of x	Value of $x^3 + x$	Bigger or smaller than 172?	
5	130	smaller	
6	222	bigger	x is between 5 and 6
5.5	171.865	smaller	x is between 5.5 and 6
5.6	181.216	bigger	x is between 5.5 and 5.6
5.55	176.503 875	bigger	x is between 5.5 and 5.55

5.5   5.55   5.6

Answer: $x = 5.5$ to 1 dp

Always set your work out in a table – it will help you to see what you are doing. The first step is to 'trap' the answer between two consecutive whole numbers. Next you must 'trap' the answer between two consecutive 1 decimal place values. Finally you must check the value halfway between these values.
To give your answer to 2 dp, you need to repeat the process to find two consecutive 2 dp values then check the value halfway between.

Chapter 34 pages 342–347

TEST YOURSELF

1. Solve the following linear equations:
   a $3x + 4 = 19$ b $2(x - 3) = 5$
   c $3(2x + 1) = 4(x + 7)$

2. Solve these simultaneous equations.
   a $x + y = 4$ b $x + 2y = 10$ c $3x + 2y = 19$
      $2x - y = 5$ $3x + y = 10$ $4x + 5y = 37$

3. Solve the following quadratic equations:
   a $x^2 + 8x + 12 = 0$ b $x^2 - 2x - 48 = 0$
   c $x^2 - 6x = 27$

4. Use trial and improvement to solve:
   a $x^2 = 214$ to 1 decimal place
   b $x^3 + 2x = 275$ to 1 decimal place
   c $x^3 = 160$ to 2 decimal places

Curved graphs

☐ Drawing curves using a table

The equation of a line is $y = 2x - 3$.

You can draw the graph of this line by finding points that lie on the line and joining them up.

x	−2	−1	0	1	2	3	4
2x	−4	−2	0	2	4	6	8
−3	−3	−3	−3	−3	−3	−3	−3
y	−7	−5	−3	−1	1	3	5

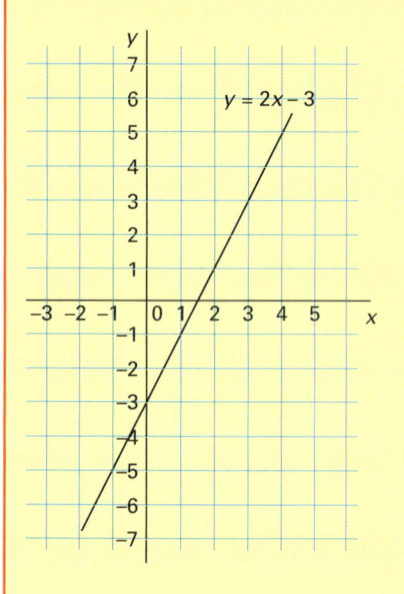

You use this method for more complicated graphs.

You still use a table of values and join up points.

A quadratic equation is one which has an x^2 in it. It must not have any other powers of x such as x^3 or $\frac{1}{x}$.

Graphs of quadratic equations are curves not straight lines.

To draw the graph of a quadratic equation you must find the co-ordinates of some points that lie on the curve.

To draw the graph of $y = x^2 + 2x - 1$ first draw a table to work out the co-ordinates.

x	−5	−4	−3	−2	−1	0	1	2	3
x^2	25	16	9	4	1	0	1	4	9
+2x	−10	−8	−6	−4	−2	0	2	4	6
−1	−1	−1	−1	−1	−1	−1	−1	−1	−1
y	14	7	2	−1	−2	−1	2	7	14

Notes

It is best to use a table to record the values.

Use a separate row for each part of the equation.
Add the rows together to get the value for y.
Use the x and y values as co-ordinates to plot your graph.

Make sure you label your graph.

Chapter 19 pages 2–4

Remember to write each part of the equation on a separate row of the table.

Once you have found the co-ordinates of points that lie on the curve you can now draw the graph.

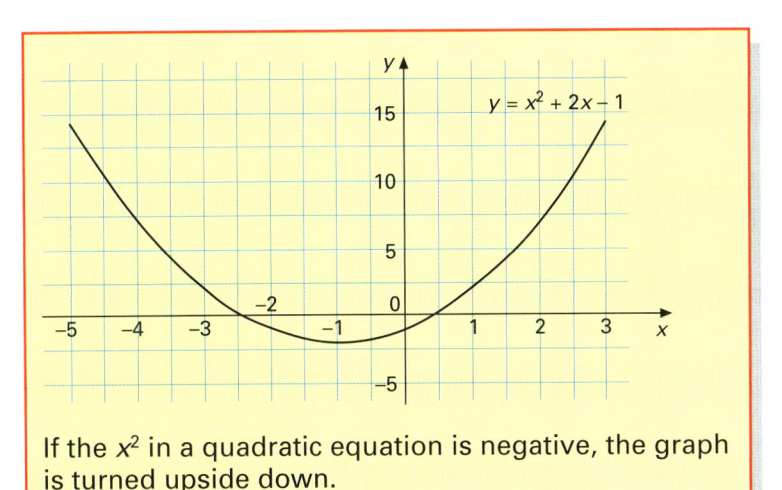

If the x^2 in a quadratic equation is negative, the graph is turned upside down.

☐ Other graphs

A **cubic** equation is one that has an x^3 in it. It must not have any higher powers of x or terms like $\frac{1}{x}$. It can have x^2 and x terms and numbers.

The graphs of cubic equations can be drawn accurately by plotting points as described for quadratic equations.

The graph of a cubic equation is a curve, but it is different from a quadratic curve. These are all cubic curves.

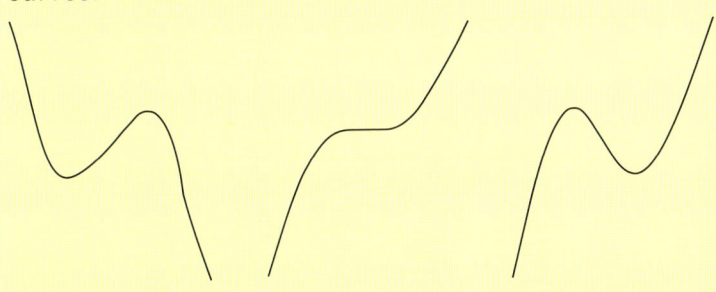

Another type of equation that has a curved graph is where the x appears on the bottom line of a fraction.

To draw the graph of $y = \frac{4}{x}$, first draw a table of values.

x	1	2	3	4	5
y	4	2	1.33	1	0.8

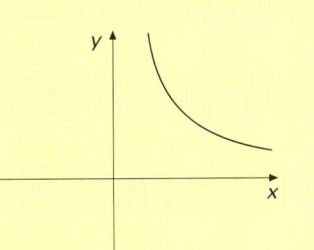

The full graph looks like this:

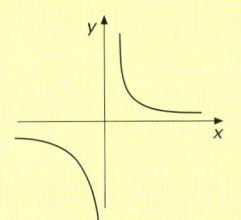

$y = \frac{4}{x}$

You get this by using negative x values.

Notes

Plot the points from the table.
Join the points with a **smooth** curve.
Remember to label your graph.

It is important to remember that $-x^2$ means find x^2 then make the answer negative.
x^2 is always a positive number so $-x^2$ will always be negative.

Chapter 19 pages 5–11 ➤

Always use a table to organise your working.

Plot the x and y values from your table and join them with a smooth curve.

$\frac{4}{x}$ means $4 \div x$.

The graph of $\frac{4}{x}$ is in two halves. The two halves do not meet because it is impossible to find a value for y when $x = 0$.

Chapter 19 pages 12–21 ➤

Sketching the graphs of quadratic equations

Factorising a quadratic equation enables you to draw a sketch of the graph. A sketch graph shows the shape of the graph and the points where it cuts the axes. You should not try to read off exact values from a sketch graph.

Example

Sketch the graph of $y = x^2 + 2x - 8$.

The curve will cut the x axis when $y = 0$.

$$x^2 + 2x - 8 = 0$$
$$(x - 2)(x + 4) = 0$$
Either $(x - 2) = 0$ or $(x + 4) = 0$
So $x = 2$ or $x = -4$

The graph cuts the x axis at $x = 2$ and $x = -4$.

The curve will cut the y axis when $x = 0$.

$$y = x^2 + 2x - 8$$
$$y = 0^2 + 2 \times 0 - 8$$
$$y = -8$$

Label the points.   Draw the graph.

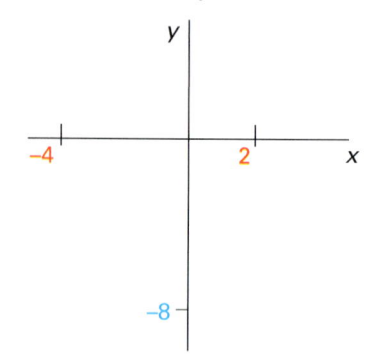

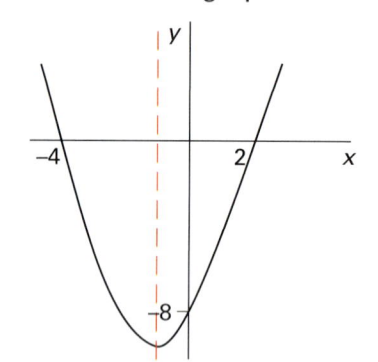

Solving equations using a graph

You can use graphs to solve different types of equations.

Example

Solve the equation: **a** $x^2 - x - 3 = 0$
b $x^2 - x - 3 = 2$

Use a table to find the co-ordinates of points that lie on the curve $y = x^2 - x - 3$.

x	-3	-2	-1	0	1	2	3
x^2	9	4	1	0	1	4	9
$-x$	3	2	1	0	-1	-2	-3
-3	-3	-3	-3	-3	-3	-3	-3
y	9	3	-1	-3	-3	-1	3

Notes

This is the sketch graph of $y = -x^2$

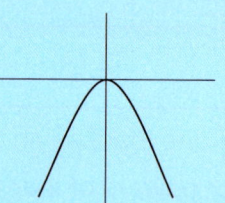

When the x^2 term is negative, the quadratic graph is turned upside down.

Draw the axes and mark the points where the curve cuts the axes.

Sketch the curve, by drawing a smooth curve through the points. The curve is always going to be symmetrical so make sure the top or bottom of the graph is halfway between your x intercepts.

The bottom of the graph is halfway between -4 and 2.

Chapter 27 pages 177–179

You need to draw your graphs as accurately as possible.
You need to read off values as carefully as you can.

$y = x^2 - x - 3$

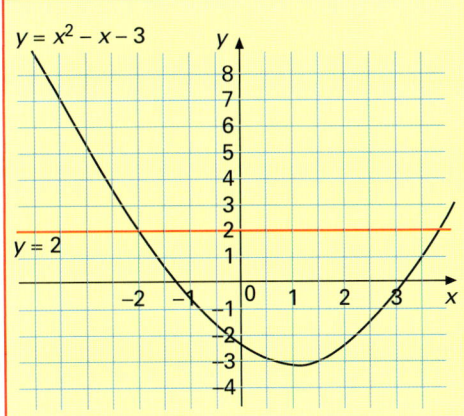

To find the solutions to $x^2 - x - 3 = 0$, you must read off the values of x where the curve cuts the x axis. These values are $x = -1.3$ and $x = -2.3$

To solve the equation $x^2 - x - 3 = 2$ you must draw the line $y = 2$ on the same axes, and read off the values of x where the graphs cross. These values are $x = -1.8$ and $x - 2.8$

Notes

A clearly drawn graph will make it easier for you to read off the values you need.

Using a sharp pencil enables you to draw clear diagrams.

☐ Solving equations using two graphs

You can solve more complicated equations by plotting graphs.

To solve equations using graphs:
1. Draw graphs of both sides of the equation.
2. Write down the x co-ordinates of the points of intersection.

Example

Solve graphically the equation $x^3 = 6 - 2x$

Draw the graph of $y = x^3$
Draw the graph of $y = 6 - 2x$

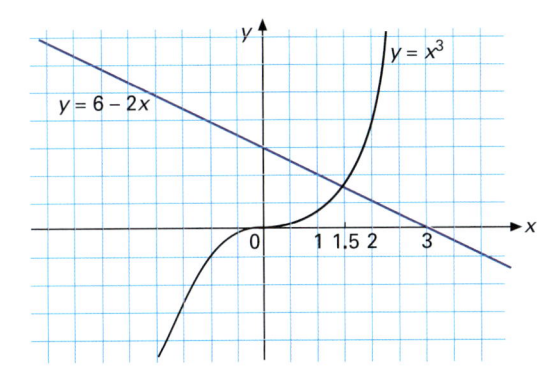

The graphs intersect at $x = 1.5$

This is the solution to the equation $x^3 = 6 - 2x$.

Draw a table to find the points that lie on the curve $y = x^3$ and $y = 6 - 2x$.

Chapter 34 pages 332–341

TEST YOURSELF

1. Draw a table of values for $y = x^2 + 3x - 1$, taking values of x from -5 to $+2$. Draw axes to fit the values in your table, and draw a graph.

2. Draw the graph of $y = x^2 - 4x + 2$. Take values of x from -3 to $+3$.

3. Sketch the graph of: $y = x^2 + 4x + 3$
Show clearly all the points where the graph cuts the axes.

4. Solve the following equations by drawing appropriate graphs.

   a $x^2 - 4x - 2 = 3$
   b $x^2 + 2x + 1 = 4$
   c $x^2 - 4x - 3 = x - 4$
   d $\frac{1}{x} = 5 - 2x$

Inequalities

☐ Showing inequalities on a number line

You can use inequalities to describe a range of numbers.

$x \leqslant 2$ means that x can be any value **less than or equal** to 2. This includes 2. On a number line, this is shown as:

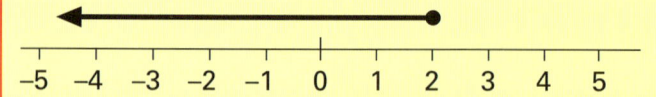

$x > 1$ means that x can be any number **greater than** 1. This does not include 1. This is shown on a number line as:

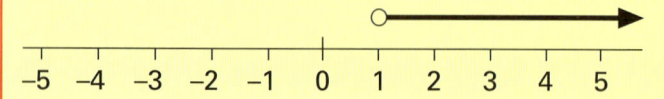

$-1 < x \leqslant 3$ means that x is **greater than** -1 and **less than or equal to** 3. This means that -1 is not included, but 3 is.

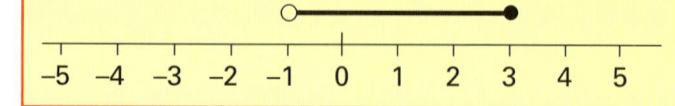

☐ Solving linear inequalities

Inequalities are solved in a similar way to equations.

Example 1
Solve $2x + 5 > 9$ Add -5 to both sides.
       $2x > 4$ Divide both sides by 2.
       $x > 2$

Example 2
Solve $4 - 2x \leqslant 3x + 1$ Add $2x$ to both sides.
       $4 \leqslant 5x + 1$ Add -1 to both sides.
       $3 \leqslant 5x$
                                    Divide both sides by 5.
       $\frac{3}{5} \leqslant x$
                                    It is usual to write the x
       $x \geqslant \frac{3}{5}$ on the left-hand side.

Example 3
Solve $8 - 3x < 23$ Subtract 8 from both sides.
       $-3x < 15$ Divide both sides by -3 and
       $x > -5$ change the direction of the
                         inequality sign.

Notes

A solid circle means that the end point is included.

The open circle means that the end point is not included.

You can add the same number to both sides of an inequality.
You can subtract the same number from both sides of an inequality.
You can multiply, or divide, both sides of an inequality by any positive number.
If you multiply, or divide, both sides of an inequality by a negative number, you must change the direction of the inequality sign.

Chapter 36 pages 372–376

TEST YOURSELF

1 Draw number lines to show these inequalities.
   a $x \geqslant 4$
   b $x < -3$
   c $1 \leqslant x < 6$
   d $-5 < x < -3$
   e $-4 \leqslant x \leqslant 2$

2 Solve these inequalities.
   a $4x - 1 > 5$
   b $3x + 2 < 7$
   c $5x - 3 \geqslant x + 7$
   d $17 - 2x > 15$
   e $3 - 5x \geqslant -2x + 6$

Solving quadratic inequalities

Example 1

Solve the inequality $2x^2 - 3 \leq 5$
$$2x^2 \leq 8$$
$$x^2 \leq 4$$

The solution is $x \geq -2$ and $x \leq 2$
This can be written $-2 \leq x \leq 2$
On a number line the solution looks like this:

```
—•————————•—
-5 -4 -3 -2 -1  0  1  2  3  4  5
```

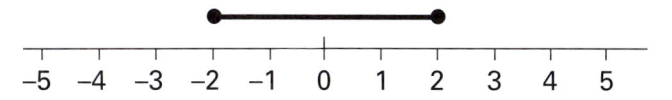

Example 2

Solve the inequality $3x^2 + 2 \geq 29$
$$3x^2 \geq 27$$
$$x^2 \geq 9$$

The solution is $x \leq -3$ and $x \geq 3$.
On a number line the solution looks like this:

```
←————•            •————→
-5 -4 -3 -2 -1  0  1  2  3  4  5
```

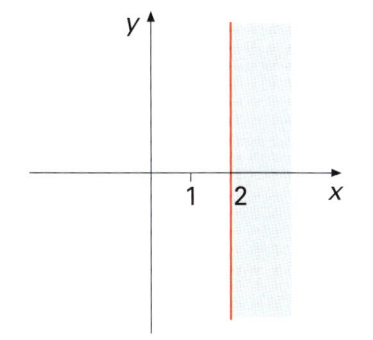

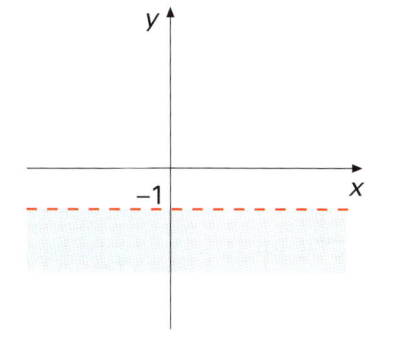

Notes

You need to find numbers that are less than 4 when squared. These are $x \leq 2$ but also $x \geq -2$.

You need to find numbers that are more than 9 when squared. These are $x \geq 3$ but also $x \geq -3$.

Chapter 36 pages 378–379

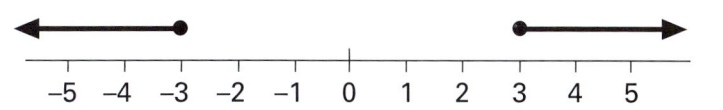

Solving inequalities using graphs

You can use graphs to solve inequalities.

The inequality $x \geq 2$ has $x = 2$ as its boundary line.
The line is included in the inequality.
All the points in the shaded region have an x co-ordinate greater than 2.

The inequality $y < 1$ has $y = -1$ as its boundary line. The line is not included in the inequality.
All the points in the shaded region have a y co-ordinate less than -1.

Notes

A graph gives you a picture of the problem. This can help you to see the answer to a problem.

If the boundary line is included in the inequality it is shown by a solid line.

If the boundary line is not included in the inequality it is shown by a dashed line.

Chapter 36 pages 380–384

TEST YOURSELF

1 Solve the following inequalities:
  a $x^2 \leq 4$
  b $x^2 \geq 16$
  c $x^2 + 5 \geq 69$
  d $3x^2 + 2 < 5$

2 Show the following inequalities on a graph:
  a $x > -1$
  b $y \leq 3$
  c $-2 \leq x < 4$
  d $0 < y \leq 3$

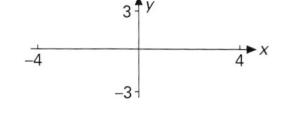

45

☐ Inequalities with two variables

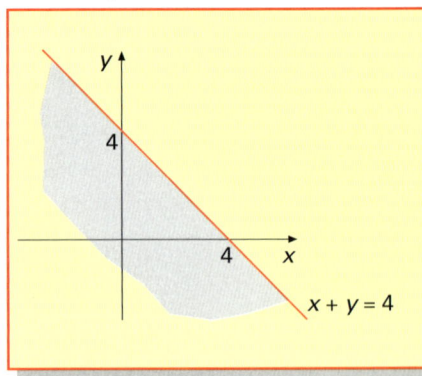

The line forming the boundary of a region may not be parallel to one of the axes. When this happens the inequality has both an *x* and a *y*.

The boundary for the region $x + y \leq 4$ is the line $x + y = 4$.

Notes

Draw the boundary line. Remember, it must be a solid line if it is included in the inequality and a dashed line if it is not included in the inequality.
To decide which side of the line to shade choose one point (the origin is a good point to choose). Substitute the co-ordinates of that point into the inequality and see if it is true. If it is true then the point you chose lies in the region you want. If the inequality is not true the shaded region must lie on the other side of the line.

☐ Using more than one inequality on the same graph

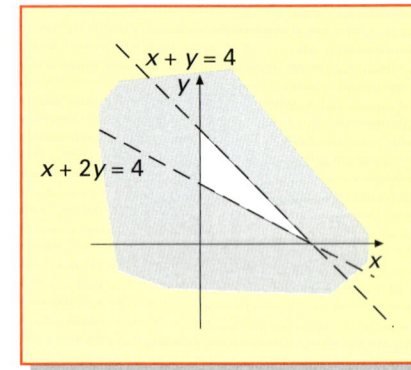

Sometimes you need more than one inequality to define a region.

The region defined by the inequalities $x \geq 0$, $y \geq 0$, $x + y < 4$ and $x + 2y > 4$ is shown by the **unshaded** area on the graph.

You must say which area represents your answer.

It is often a good idea to shade the region you do **not** want. This means that the unshaded region represents your answer.

Chapter 36 pages 385–388

☐ Using inequalities to solve problems

Many real-life problems can be solved by using inequalities.

John wants to buy a combination of chart singles on CD and tape. CDs cost £5 and tapes cost £4. He has £30 to spend altogether.

He wants to buy at least one CD and at least 2 tapes. He is prepared to spend all of his money. How many CDs and tapes can he buy?

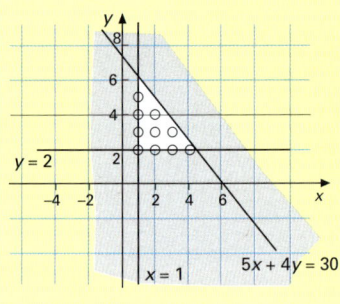

Each point that is circled is a possible solution to John's problem.

He can buy 4 CDs and 2 tapes, for example.

The number of CDs bought can be represented by x, and the number of tapes bought represented by y.
Using the information given you can write down three inequalities.
$x \geq 1$
$y \geq 2$
$5x + 4y \leq 30$

Chapter 36 pages 388–391

TEST YOURSELF

1 Draw graphs to show the following inequalities:
  a $x + y < 5$
  b $x + 2y \geq 8$
  c $2x + 3y \leq 12$
  d $y < x$

2 Draw graphs to show the regions defined by these sets of inequalities.
  a $x \geq 0$, $y \geq 0$, $x + y < 6$
  b $x > 4$, $y \geq -5$, $x + y \leq 5$
  c $y > x$, $x > -2$, $x + 2y \leq 6$

Practice questions

1 a Write down **i** the 8th term and **ii** the *n*th term of this sequence:

    1   5   9   13   17   ... (2)

  b Use your answer to **a** to write down the *n*th term of this sequence:

    1   25   81   169   289   ... (1)

OCR, 1999, Paper 1664/4

2 It takes Samir 8 minutes to fill his bath.
The bath fills at 25 litres per minute for the first 2 minutes.
The rate of flow is 15 litres per minute for the next 2 minutes.
In the last 4 minutes, the bath fills at only 5 litres per minute.

  a Copy the grid and shown this information on it. (4)

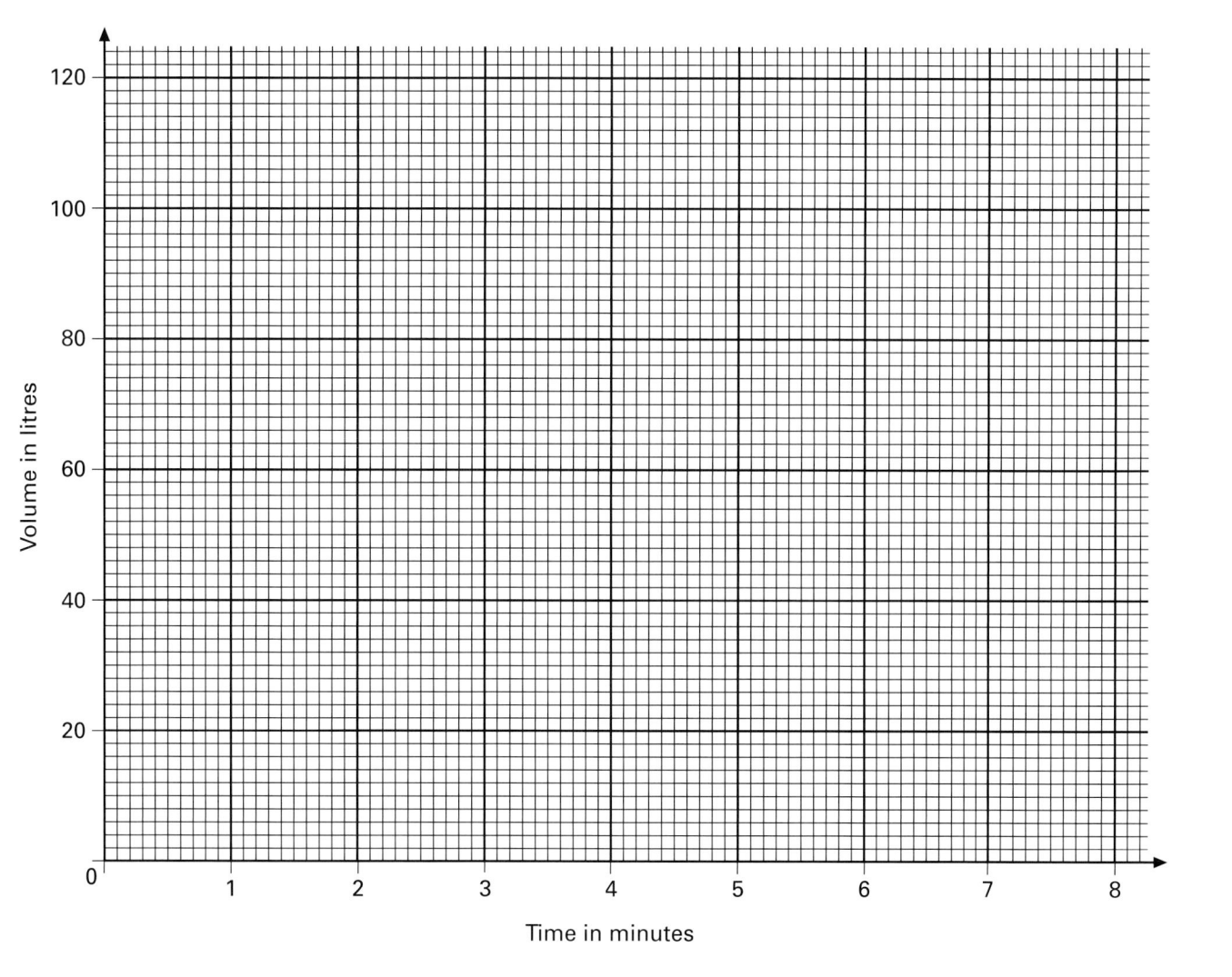

  b Calculate the average rate of flow of the water in filling Samir's bath. (2)

OCR, 1999, Paper 1664/4

47

3

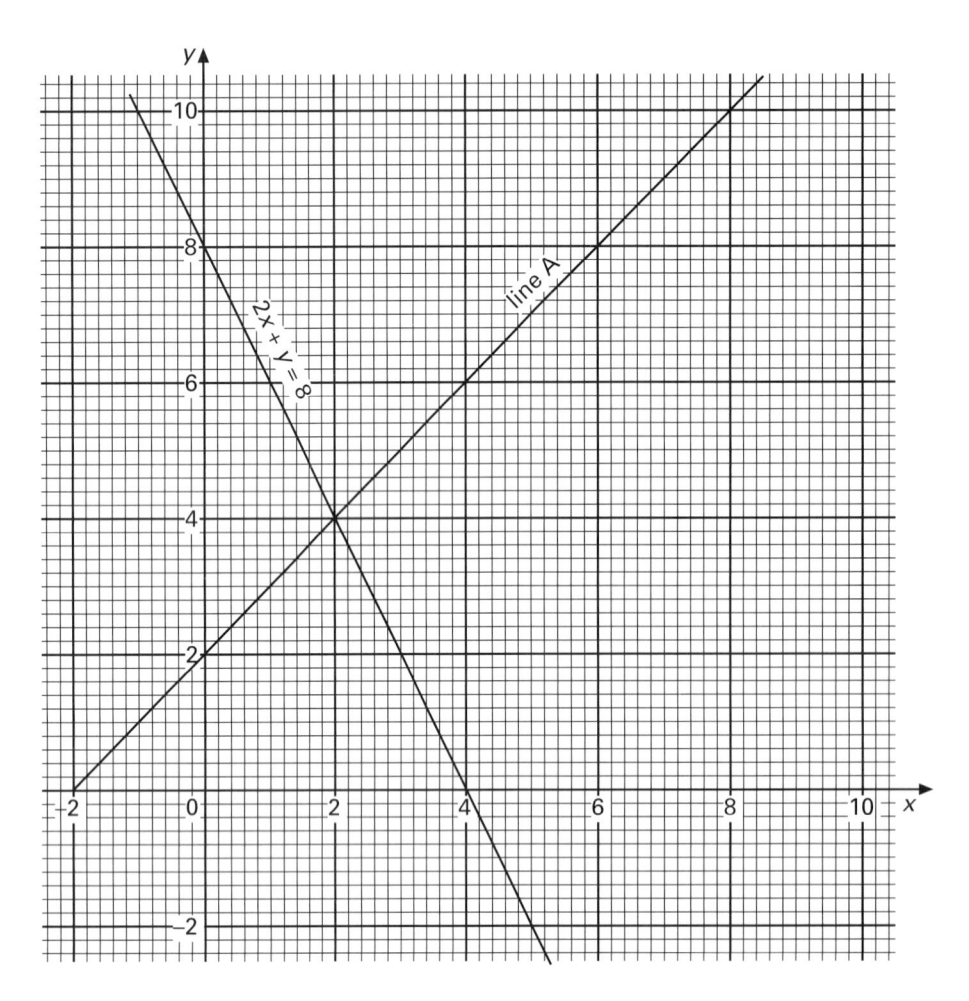

a What is the equation of the line A drawn on the grid? (2)

b Draw the line $x + 2y = 6$ on a copy of the grid. (2)

c Hence solve the simultaneous equations

$2x + y = 8$
$x + 2y = 6.$ (2)

OCR, 1999, Paper 1662/3

4 a Solve the inequality

$$9n = 1 < 14n - 2.$$ (3)

b Multiply out the brackets and simplify

$$(x + 3)(2x - 1).$$ (2)

c Factorise

$$x^2 - 3x - 4.$$ (2)

d Rearrange the formula $s = \frac{1}{2}gt^2$ to make t the subject. (2)

OCR, 1999, Paper 1664/4

5   ○☆○   ○☆☆○☆☆○   ○☆☆☆○☆☆☆○☆☆☆○☆☆☆○
    Pattern 1   Pattern 2   Pattern 3

and so on.

Each pattern in this sequence consists of circles and stars.

a Copy and complete the table:

Pattern	Number of circles	Number of stars
1	2	1
2	3	4
3	4	9
4		
5		

(4)

b i How many circles are in Pattern 20? (1)

  ii How many stars are in Pattern 20? (2)

c One of these Pattern has 9 circles.

How many stars are in this Pattern? (2)

d For Pattern n, write down in terms of n,

  i the number of circles (1)

  ii the number of stars. (1)

NICCEA, 1999, Paper G60–4I

6 a Solve the inequality $3(x - 7) < 1 - 2(1 + x)$ where x is an integer greater than zero.
Illustrate your solution on a copy of the number line below.

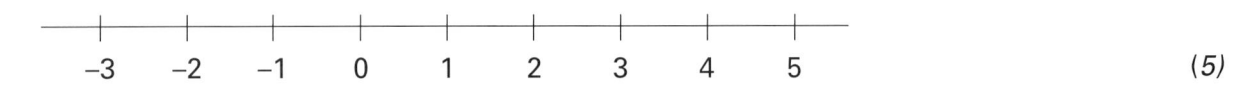

$$-3 \quad -2 \quad -1 \quad 0 \quad 1 \quad 2 \quad 3 \quad 4 \quad 5$$

(5)

b Solve $\frac{1}{4}(x + 2) - \frac{1}{2}(2x - 1) = 4$ (4)

NICCEA, 1999, Paper G60–3I

49

7 There are three values of x which are solutions to the equation

$$x^3 - 22x + 24 = 0$$

a Show that $x = 4$ is a solution to the equation. *(2)*

b A second solution lies between 1 and 2.
Use trial and improvement to find this second positive solution of x.
Give your answer correct to 1 decimal place.

x	$x^3 - 22x + 24$
1	$1^3 - 22 \times 1 + 24 = 3$
2	$2^3 - 22 \times 2 + 24 = -12$

(3)

c Part of the graph of $y = x^3 - 22x + 24$ is shown below.

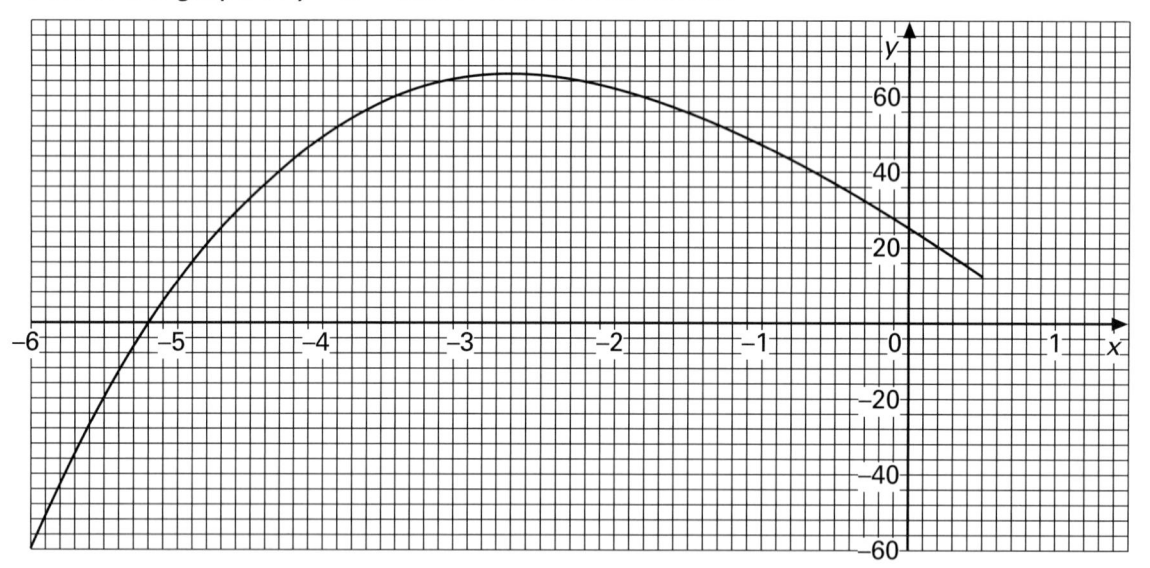

Use the graph to write down the third solution of $x^3 - 22x + 24 = 0$ *(1)*

AQA, 1999, Paper 2291

8 a Solve the inequality

$$3x + 4 \leq 7$$ *(2)*

b i Solve the inequality

$$3x + 11 \geq 4 - 2x$$ *(2)*

ii If x is an integer what is the smallest possible value of x? *(1)*

AQA, 1999, Paper 2292

3 Shape and space

- [ ] **Transformations**
- [ ] **Trigonometry**
- [ ] **Units of measurement**
- [ ] **Perimeter and circumference**
- [ ] **Pythagoras**
- [ ] **Areas, nets and surface areas**
- [ ] **Angles**
- [ ] **Volume**
- [ ] **Dimensional analysis**
- [ ] **Symmetry**
- [ ] **Loci**

Practice questions

Transformations

☐ Congruence

Two shapes are **congruent** if they are identical. They must be exactly the same size *and* shape.

Example

These two shapes are congruent. They are exactly the same size and shape.

This square is not congruent to the other two. It is not the same size.

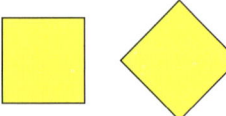

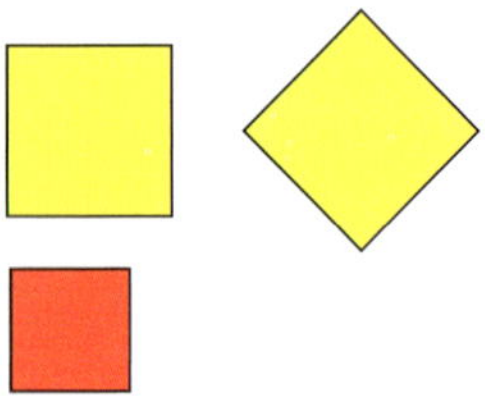

☐ Tessellation

A **tessellation** is a pattern made by repeating the same shape over and over again. There must not be any gaps.

This tessellation is made from quadrilaterals.

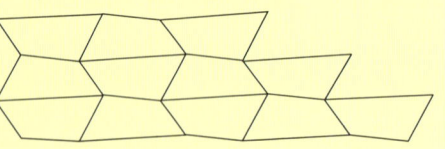

☐ Translations

A translation is a movement in a straight line. The image must look exactly the same as the object. You can show translations with column vectors.

A translation of 3 right and 4 up is written $\begin{pmatrix} 3 \\ 4 \end{pmatrix}$.

☐ Inverse of a translation

The inverse of a translation takes you back to where you started from. The inverse of $\begin{pmatrix} 3 \\ 4 \end{pmatrix}$ is $\begin{pmatrix} -3 \\ -4 \end{pmatrix}$.

Example

Triangle A'B'C' is a translation of triangle ABC.

ABC has been translated by the column vector $\begin{pmatrix} -4 \\ -1 \end{pmatrix}$.

The inverse of this translation is $\begin{pmatrix} 4 \\ 1 \end{pmatrix}$.

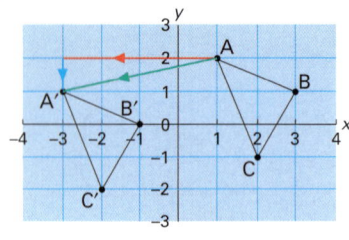

Notes

Remember that congruent is another word for identical.

You can see that shapes do not have to be the same way round to be congruent.

All quadrilaterals tessellate.

All triangles tessellate. You can turn one over to make a quadrilateral with the two triangles like in this picture.

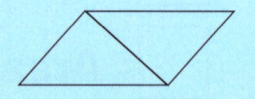

The shape that you start with is called the **object**.
The shape that you get after you do a transformation is called the **image**.

The sign of each number in a column vector gives the direction of movement. This matches the labelling on the axes.

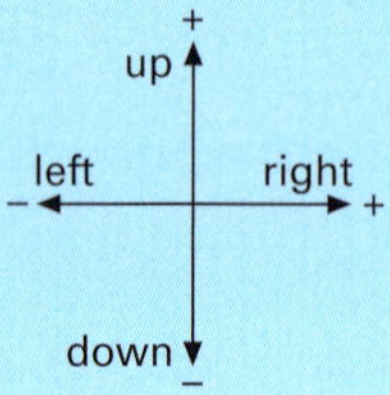

It is best to look at the movement of an individual point to find a column vector for a translation.

The special feature of a translation is that it always has the same size image in the same orientation as the object.

TEST YOURSELF

1 Draw a tessellation for each of these shapes.
   a   b 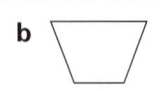   c

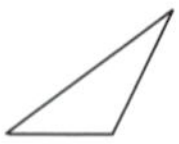

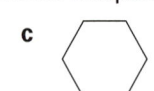

2 Use column vectors to describe these transformations.
   a A to B   b D to C
   c A to D   d C to B

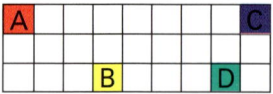

☐ Reflections

When you reflect an object in a line every point moves the same distance on the other side of the line.
Every point moves across at right angles to the mirror.

Example

Triangle A'B'C' is the reflection of triangle ABC in the line x = −4.

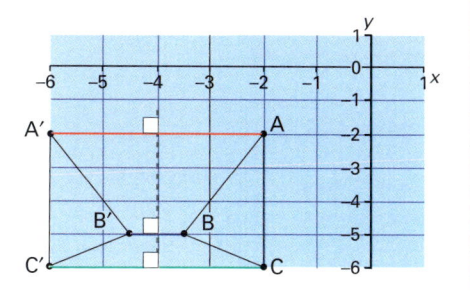

☐ Inverse of a reflection

The inverse of a reflection is the same reflection.

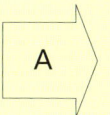

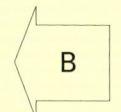

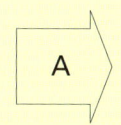

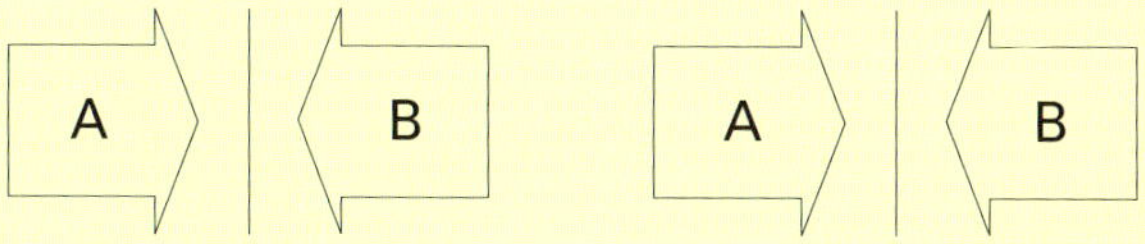

The reflection of A in the line gives B.

The reflection of B in the line gives A.

☐ Rotations

A rotation turns a shape around a fixed point. This point is called the centre of rotation.

To rotate a shape about a point:

(1) You need to know the angle and the direction of turn.
(2) Trace the shape and the centre.
(3) Put a cross at the centre.
(4) Put your pencil on the centre of the rotation and rotate the tracing paper.
(5) Draw the shape in its new position.

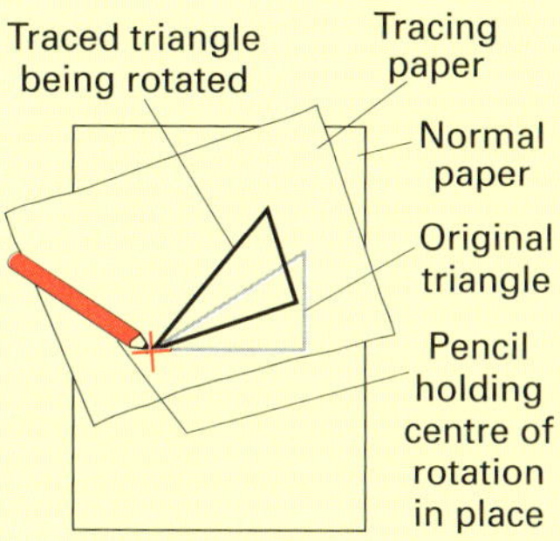

☐ Inverse of a rotation

The inverse of a rotation is another rotation.
It has the same centre and angle but the opposite direction of rotation.

So the inverse of a rotation of 90° anticlockwise about (−2,1) is a rotation of 90° clockwise about (−2,1).

Notes

Make sure that you ask for tracing paper if you want to use it in your exam.

Think of the line you are reflecting in as a mirror.

Notice how AA', BB', and CC' are all bisected (cut in half) by the mirror line.

This is the special feature of a reflection. You don't do **exactly** the same thing to get the inverse with any other transformation.

When you describe a rotation you must give these **three** things:
- the centre – give this using co-ordinates
- the angle that you rotate the shape
- the direction that you turn – clockwise or anticlockwise

A cross at the centre is helpful to see rotations of 90° and 180° when the cross will look the same as when it started.

The special features of a rotation are that:

(1) the vertices of the image are always a different way round from the object.*
This means you can't translate an object onto its rotated image.

(2) if you letter the vertices, they retain the same clockwise order round the shape. This distinguishes it from a reflection.

* Unless you rotate through full turns!

☐ Enlargements

> This transformation changes the size of the object.
>
> To describe an enlargement you give two things:
> - the centre
> - the scale factor.

Notes

This is the special feature of an enlargement.
It is the only transformation that changes the size of the object.

Example
Enlarge the triangle DEF with scale factor 3, centre (1, 2).

Start from the centre (1, 2).
Draw and measure the line CD.

Draw CD′ so that it is 3 times as long as CD.

Repeat for the lines CE and CF to get CE′ and CF′.

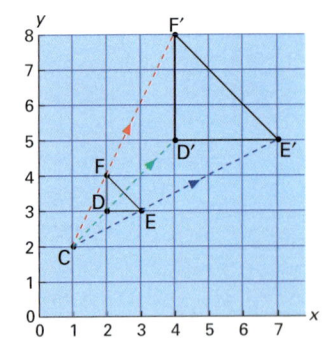

When the centre of enlargement is at the origin, to calculate the image co-ordinates, multiply all the object co-ordinates by the scale factor.
So for an enlargement, centre (0, 0), scale factor 4, the image of the point (2, 3) is the point (8, 12).

☐ Inverse of an enlargement

> An inverse reverses the original enlargement.
>
> For an original enlargement and its inverse:
> - They have the same centre of enlargement.
> - They have reciprocal scale factors.
>
> So if the scale factor of the original enlargement is k, the scale factor of the inverse is $\frac{1}{k}$.

The inverse takes the image back into the object.

If the original scale factor is $\frac{a}{b}$,
The inverse scale factor is $\frac{b}{a}$.

An enlargement with a scale factor less than 1 reduces the size of the object.

Example
An enlargement has a scale factor of: **a** 6   **b** $1\frac{1}{2}$
Find the scale factor of the inverse for each enlargement.

a The reciprocal of 6 is $\frac{1}{6}$.
b $2\frac{1}{2}$ is $\frac{5}{2}$, so its reciprocal is $\frac{2}{5}$.

You make $2\frac{1}{2}$ an improper fraction.

> Chapter 1 pages 7–16

TEST YOURSELF

1 a Copy the diagram.
  b Reflect the pentagon RSTUV in the line $y = x$.

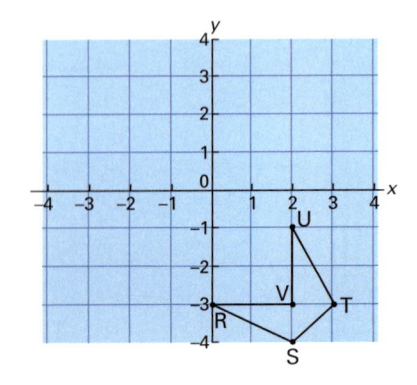

2 A quadrilateral has co-ordinates A (2, 0), B (4, 0), C (4, 4) and D (2, 2).
  a Draw axes for values of x and y from 0 to 10.
  b Enlarge ABCD with scale factor $2\frac{1}{2}$, centre (0, 2).
  c Write down the scale factor of the inverse.

3 a Copy the diagram in question **1** again.
  b Rotate the pentagon RSTUV through 90° anticlockwise about the origin.
  c Fully describe the inverse of this rotation.

☐ Similar triangles

Similar objects are the same shape but different sizes. Two objects are similar if one is an enlargement of the other.
If two triangles are similar, they have these properties:
- All three pairs of angles are equal.
- All the pairs of corresponding sides are in the same ratio so $\frac{a}{p}=\frac{b}{q}=\frac{c}{r}$.

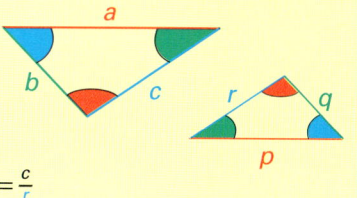

Example

Find the lengths marked with letters.

The scale factor from ABC to CDE is clearly more than 1.
It is $DE \div BA = 6 \div 1\frac{1}{2} = \frac{6}{1} \times \frac{2}{3} = 4$
CE corresponds to CA so $CE = 4 \times 1\frac{1}{4} = 5$ m
CB corresponds to CD so $CB = 3 \div 4 = \frac{3}{4}$ m

☐ Combined transformations

Sometimes shapes are mapped into position by more than one transformation. This can be done in stages.

Example

Shape A maps to shape B by a reflection in the *y* axis.
Shape B maps to shape C by a reflection in the *x* axis.

There is a single transformation that maps A to C. It is a rotation of 180° about the origin.

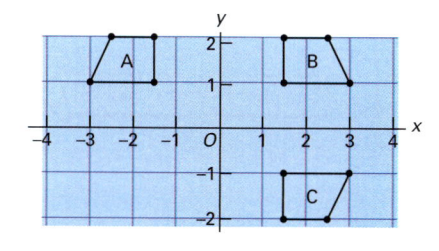

Notes

If similar objects are the same size they are usually called congruent.

There are four favourite types of triangles questions with examiners. They are:

(1)

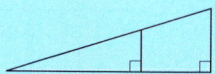

(2) All 3 triangles (yes there **are** 3!) are similar.

(3) Another type of parallel lines question. It can be very tricky.

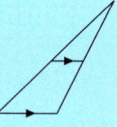

(4) The one in the example.

If you are asked to prove two triangles are similar, always give your reasons.
You might be expected to do fractions like this in a non-calculator paper.

When looking for single transformations to replace a combined transformation, be systematic. Go through all the alternatives: translation, reflection, rotation, enlargement. Remember the special features of each type.

Chapter 1 pages 17–20

TEST YOURSELF

1. **a** Explain why triangles ABC and ADE are similar.
   b Work out the lengths marked with letters.

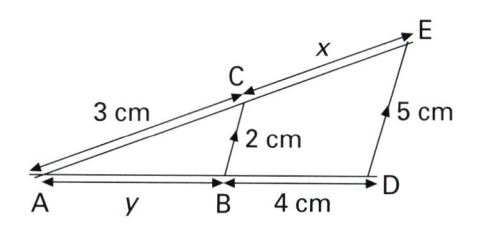

2. **a** Copy the diagram.
   b Reflect DEFG in the *y* axis. Label this D'E'F'G'.
   c Rotate D'E'F'G' 180° about the origin. Label this D"E"F"G".
   d Describe in full the single transformation that maps DEFG to D"E"F"G".

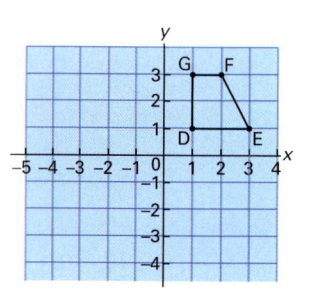

55

Trigonometry

☐ SOH CAH TOA

SOH CAH TOA stands for

$$\sin x = \frac{\text{Opposite}}{\text{Hypotenuse}}$$

$$\cos x = \frac{\text{Adjacent}}{\text{Hypotenuse}}$$

$$\tan x = \frac{\text{Opposite}}{\text{Adjacent}}$$

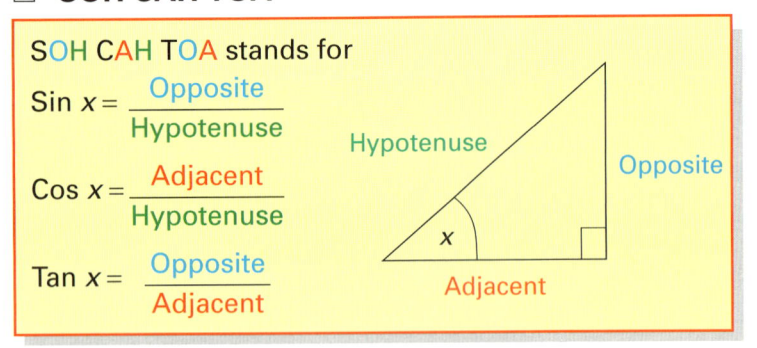

☐ Finding an angle

Write out S̶O̶H C̶A̶H̶ T̶O̶A̶

Cross out the sides you know. You use the formula where both sides are crossed out.

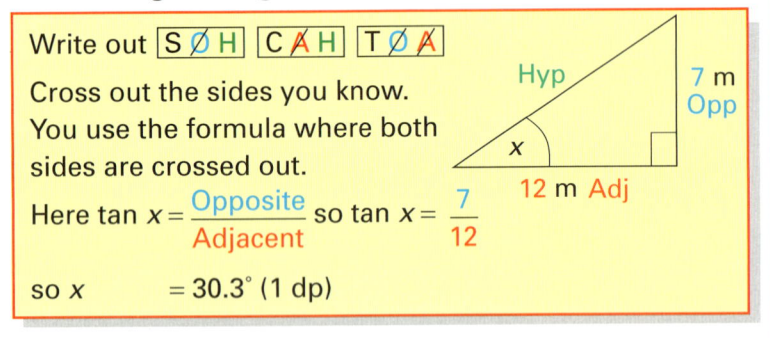

Here $\tan x = \frac{\text{Opposite}}{\text{Adjacent}}$ so $\tan x = \frac{7}{12}$

so $x = 30.3°$ (1 dp)

☐ Finding a side

Write out S̶O̶H̶ C̶A̶H̶ T̶O̶A̶

Cross out the side you know and the side you want. You use the formula where both sides are crossed out.

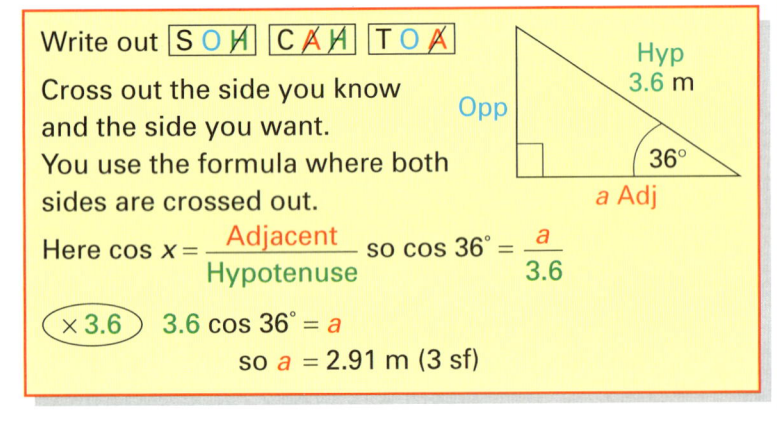

Here $\cos x = \frac{\text{Adjacent}}{\text{Hypotenuse}}$ so $\cos 36° = \frac{a}{3.6}$

(× 3.6) $3.6 \cos 36° = a$

so $a = 2.91$ m (3 sf)

Notes

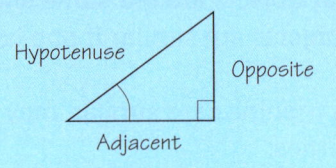

Any right-angled triangle can have its sides labelled like this. Opposite means opposite the angle you have or are trying to find.

It might help you to remember SOHCAHTOA because it rhymes with Krakatoa. Krakatoa was an island that was completely blown out of the Pacific in the 19th century by a gigantic volcanic explosion.

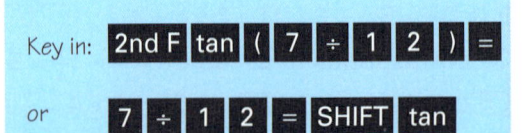

Key in: | 2nd F | tan | (| 7 | ÷ | 1 | 2 |) | = |

or | 7 | ÷ | 1 | 2 | = | SHIFT | tan |

You could do a quick scale drawing to check your answer.

(× 3.6) means 'multiply both sides by 3.6'

Key in: | 3 | . | 6 | × | cos | 3 | 6 | = |

or | 3 | . | 6 | × | 3 | 6 | cos | = |

Again, you could do a quick scale drawing to check your answer.

Chapter 14 pages 302–317

TEST YOURSELF

1 Find the labelled angles in these triangles. Give your answers to the nearest degree.

a 5 mm, 8 mm, angle a

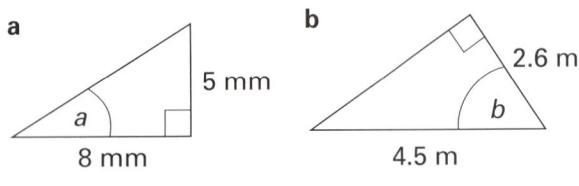

b 2.6 m, 4.5 m, angle b

c 12 cm, 7 cm, angle c

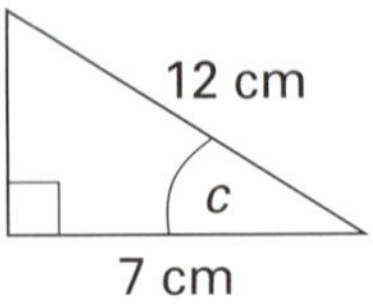

2 Find the length of the marked side in each of these triangles.

a 72 cm, 27°, side d

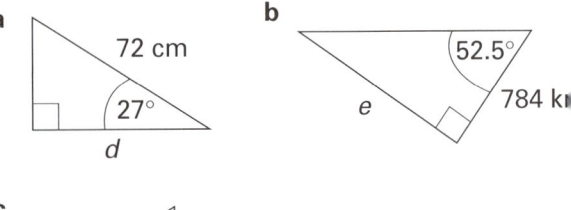

b 52.5°, 784 km, side e

c 9.6 m, 32°, side f

56

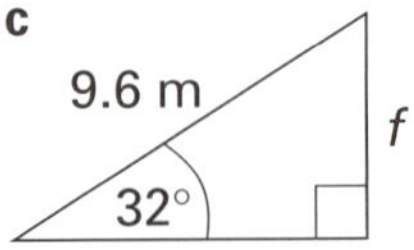

☐ Isosceles and equilateral triangles

You can split both of these into two right-angled triangles.

Notes

You can split an equilateral triangle in the same sort of way.

You have a big advantage with an equilateral triangle. You know that all its sides are equal. You also know that all its angles are 60°.

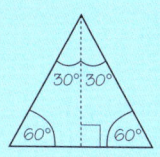

Example
Find the height of this triangle.
Split the triangle.
Label the height h.

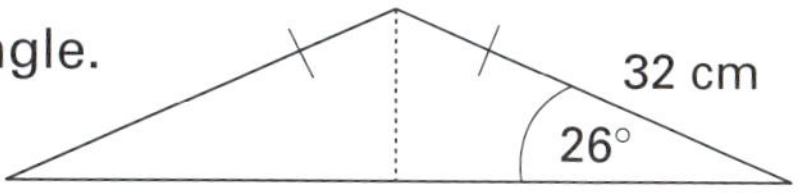

Then $\frac{h}{32} = \sin 26°$

So h = 32 sin 26°
 = 14.0 cm (3 sf)

Chapter 14 pages 315–317

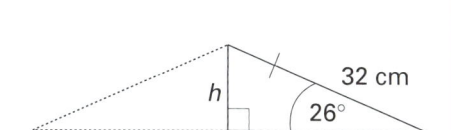

☐ Angles of elevation and depression

For elevation it is the angle you look up from the horizontal.

For depression it is the angle you look down from the horizontal.

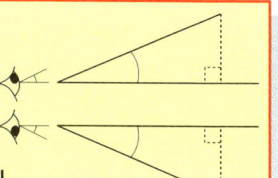

If you are elevated (pleased) your head tends to go up!
If you are depressed about something your head tends to go down!

☐ Finding the hypotenuse

To find out the hypotenuse marked h in this triangle.
Write out S O H̶   C A H̶   T O A̶

Cross out the side you know.
Cross out the hypotenuse.

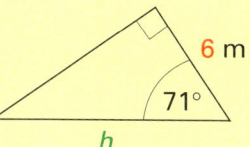

You use the formula where both sides are crossed out.

$\cos 71° = \frac{6}{h}$ multiplying by h, h cos 71° = 6

dividing by cos 71°, $h = \frac{6}{\cos 71°}$ so   h = 18.4 (3 sf)

You need to make h the subject of the formula. Here it is a denominator, so multiply by h on both sides.

You need to divide both sides by cos 71° to get h on its own.

Key in

or

| 6 | ÷ | cos | 7 | 1 | = |

| 6 | ÷ | 7 | 1 | cos | = |

TEST YOURSELF

1 Find the height of this triangle. (1.4 m, 17°)

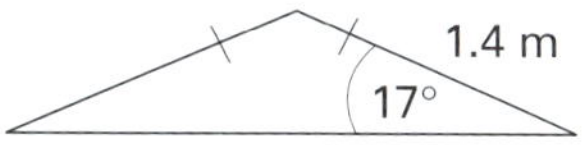

2 Find the length of the hypotenuse in this triangle. (27°, 6.5 km)

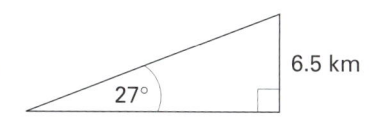

3 Find: **a** BC
        b AB
  (27 m, 66°, A, B, C)

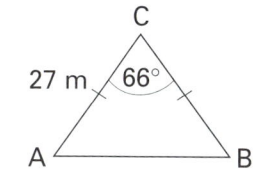

4 The angle of depression of a boat from the top of a cliff is 21°. The boat is 120 m from the base of the cliff. Find the direct distance of the boat from the top of the cliff.

Units of measurement

☐ Metric units

The conversions you need to know are

Length	Mass	Capacity
1 cm = 10 mm	1 g = 1000 mg	1 ℓ = 100 cℓ
1 m = 100 cm	1 kg = 1000 g	1 ℓ = 1000 mℓ
1 km = 1000 m	1 t = 1000 kg	

Examples

a Change 320 cm to m. **b** Change 7.4 km to m.
c Change 4650 g to kg. **d** Change 2.4 t to kg.
e Change 2.7 ℓ to mℓ. **f** Change 75 cℓ to ℓ.

a Each metre is 100 cm.
320 cm = 320 ÷ 100 = 3.2 m
c Each kilogram is 1000 g.
4650 g = 4650 ÷ 1000 = 4.65 kg
e Each litre is 1000 mℓ.
2.7 ℓ = 2.7 × 1000 = 2700 mℓ

b Each kilometre is 1000 m.
7.4 km = 7.4 × 1000 = 7400 m
d Each tonne is 1000 kg.
2.4 t = 2.4 × 1000 = 2400 kg
f Each litre is 100 cℓ.
75 cℓ = 75 ÷ 100 = 0.75 ℓ

☐ Imperial units

These are some of the Imperial units in daily use.

Length	Mass	Capacity
1 foot = 12 inches	1 pound = 16 ounces	1 gallon = 8 pints
1 yard = 3 feet	1 stone = 14 pounds	
1 mile = 1760 yards		

Examples

a Change 60 in to ft. **b** Change 21 yd to ft.
c Change 5 lb to oz. **d** Change 72 pts to gal.

a Each foot is 12 inches.
60 in = 60 ÷ 12 = 5 ft
c Each pound is 16 oz.
5 lb = 5 × 16 = 80 oz

b Each yard is 3 feet.
21 yd = 21 × 3 = 63 ft
d Each gallon is 8 pints.
72 pt = 72 ÷ 8 = 9 gal

Notes

Make sure you have a good idea of the size of these units before doing conversions.

Chapter 17 pages 365–373

Chapter 30 pages 232–238

Always state the conversion before you do any multiplying or dividing. Ask yourself if the conversion looks sensible from your everyday knowledge of units.

Always ask yourself if there will be more or less when you have changed units.

For example if you change 5 cm to mm there will obviously be more in mm. This means you will need to multiply.

On the other hand if you change 50 mm to cm, you will obviously have less in cm. This means you will need to divide.

All these common imperial units have abbreviations. They are:

length	inch (in)
	foot (ft)
	yard (yd)
mass	ounces (oz)
	pound (lb)
	stone (st)
capacity	pints (pt)
	gallons (gal)

TEST YOURSELF

1 Change each of these to the units shown.
  a 4 m to cm   **b** 6.2 km to m
  c 85 mm to cm   **d** 7800 m to km
  e 4800 mg to g   **f** 2.9 g to mg
  g 94 000 kg to t **h** 5.85 kg to g
  i 45 cℓ to ℓ   **j** 2300 mℓ to ℓ
  k 2.5 ℓ to cℓ   **l** 0.45 ℓ to mℓ

2 Change each of these to the units shown.
  a 24 in into ft   **b** 12 ft into in
  c 30 yd into ft   **d** 10 ft into yd
  e 5280 yd into miles **f** 5 miles into yd
  g 10 lb into oz   **h** 24 oz into lb
  i 5 st into lb   **j** 49 lb into st
  k 20 pt into gal   **l** 96 pt into gal

Changing between metric and imperial units

You can use conversion numbers for this.
From imperial, × by the conversion number to get metric. From metric, ÷ by the conversion number to get imperial.

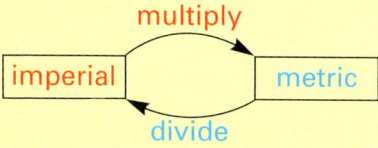

imperial →(multiply)→ metric
metric →(divide)→ imperial

For **lengths** use these conversion numbers.
1 in is about 2.5 cm.   1 ft is about 30 cm.
1 yd is about 90 cm.   1 mile is about 1.6 km.

For **masses** use these conversion numbers.
1 oz is about 30 g.   1 lb is about 450 g.
1 st is about 6.5 kg.

For **capacities** use these conversion numbers.
1 pt is about 600 mℓ.   1 gal is about 4.5 ℓ.

Examples
Convert: **a** 240 grams to ounces **b** 12 gallons to litres

a 30 g in every ounce
You need to divide.
240 ÷ 30 = 8 oz

b 1 gallon is about 4.5 ℓ.
You need to multiply.
12 × 4.5 = 54 ℓ

Estimating lengths, masses and capacities

To estimate these, it helps to think of objects you know well. Some examples are:

About 1lb or 0.45 kg (Baked Beans)

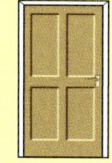

About 2 m or 6 ft (door)

About 0.6 ℓ or 1 pint (bottle)

Example
Estimate the height of a double decker bus.

A bus must have enough room for people to stand up on both floors. So it must be at least 2 m for each floor. It also has about $\frac{1}{2}$ m ground clearance.

A good estimate is 5 m.

Notes

Remember   imperial
m
u
l
t
i
p
l
y

(only imperial and multiply have 'l's in).

Remember that an adult is a bit less than 2 m tall. An 800 m race is slightly less than a km. A standard size tin of baked beans is about $\frac{1}{2}$ kg whereas a baked bean is about a gram. A car is about a tonne. A tall carton of milk is a litre and a centimetre cube of milk is a millilitre.

Chapter 30 pages 236–238

TEST YOURSELF

1 Convert each of these into the units shown.
 a 4 in into cm
 b 150 cm into ft
 c 16 km into miles
 d 60 cm into in
 e 4 oz into g
 f 900 g into lb
 g 10 st into kg
 h 240 g into oz
 i 5 pt into mℓ
 j 6 gal into ℓ
 k 2400 mℓ into pt
 l 90 ℓ into gal

2 Estimate the following
 a The height of a milk float in metres
 b The height of a room in feet
 c The mass of a typical pair of shoes in pounds
 d The mass of a mince pie in grams
 e The capacity of an athlete's drink bottle in litres

59

Perimeter and circumference

☐ Perimeter

> This is the total distance around the outside of a shape.

Example
Find the perimeter of these shapes.

a
   8 cm
3 cm [rectangle]

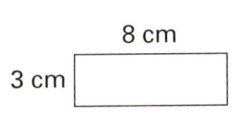

b
   5 cm
3 cm   4 cm
       9 cm

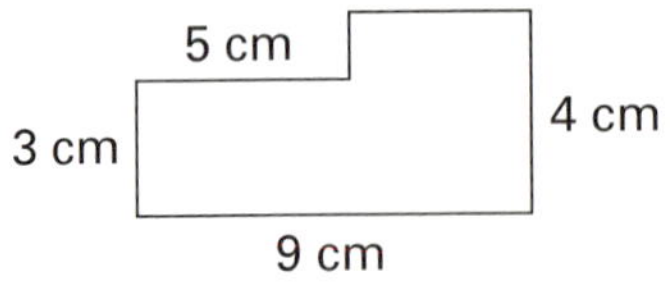

a This shape is a rectangle.
Mark the start with an arrow.
Mark on the other 2 sides.

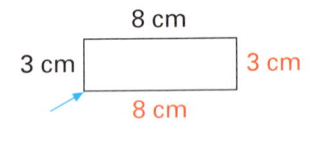

   8 cm
3 cm   3 cm
   8 cm

Perimeter = 3 + 8 + 3 + 8
         = 22 cm

b Mark on any missing sides.
Mark the start with an arrow.
Now add up all the sides.

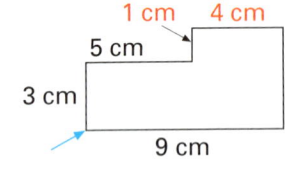

        1 cm   4 cm
   5 cm
3 cm   4 cm
        9 cm

Perimeter = 3 + 5 + 1 + 4 + 4 + 9
         = 26 cm

☐ Circumference of a circle

> The circumference is the distance round the edge of a circle.
> It is '3 and a little bit' times the diameter.
> This number is called π. It is very near to 3.14.
> The formula is **circumference = π × diameter**

Example
Find the circumference of a circle with a radius of 10 cm.

The diameter is 2 × the radius,
so the diameter is 2 × 10 = 20 cm

circumference = π × diameter
So circumference = π × 20 = 62.831....
                = 62.8 cm (1 dp)

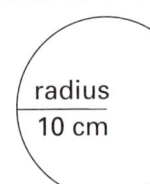

radius
10 cm

Notes

It is a good idea to mark where you start from with an arrow. The arrow reminds you not to miss a side out. It also helps to prevent you counting a side twice.

A common mistake when finding the perimeter of a rectangle is to forget to put in any missing sides.

Do *not* include any internal measurements.

You could find the perimeter of the rectangle by doing   2 × 3 + 2 × 8
                    =   6 + 16
                    =   22 cm

The circumference is very roughly 3 times the diameter. You can use this to check that your answer is about right.

You may remember that π is a never-ending number. Its decimal places go on forever! You can get a very good value from your calculator.

You can write this as a formula $C = \pi d$

You key in [π] [×] [2] [0] [=]

Chapter 17 pages 358–363

TEST YOURSELF

1 Find the perimeter of these shapes in metres.

a
25 cm [hexagon]

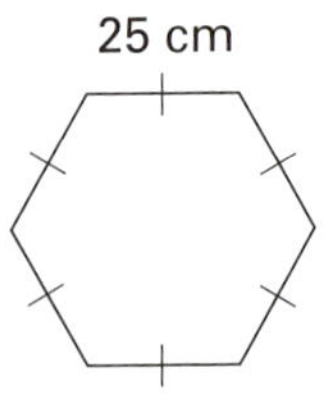

b
   2.45 m
              50 cm
0.8 m
       1.63 m

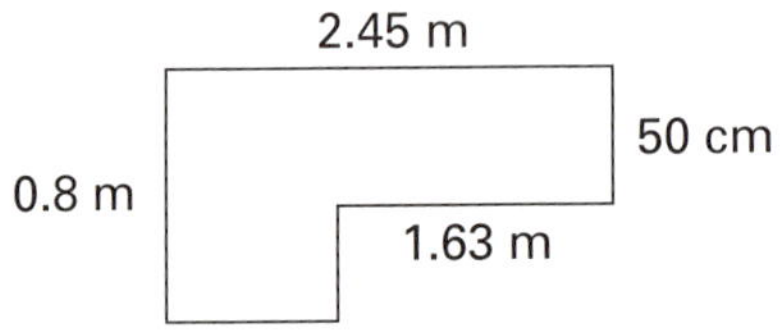

2 Find the circumference of these circles. Round your answers to 1 dp.

a 25 cm

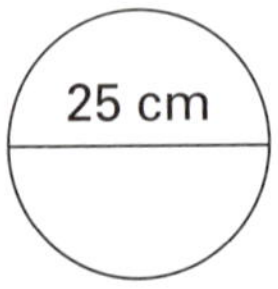

b 5.4 m

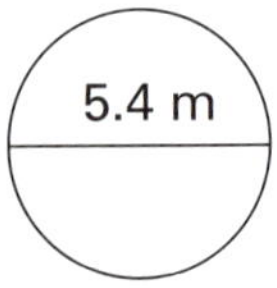

c 2.7 cm

Finding the diameter or radius of a circle

Suppose you have the circumference of a circle and you need to find the diameter. You can use the formula $d = \frac{C}{\pi}$

Notes

This means that

$$\text{diameter} = \frac{\text{circumference}}{\pi}$$

Example
Find the diameter of a circle whose circumference is 24 m.
Substituting into $d = \frac{C}{\pi}$, $d = \frac{24}{3.14...}$ so $d = 7.6$ cm (1 dp)

You may want to find the radius from the circumference.
To do this, find the diameter then divide by 2.

Finding perimeters involving parts of circles

To find the perimeter of shapes like these, split them into straight lines and curved lines.

To find the perimeter of this shape, first work out any missing lengths.

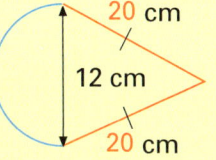

20 cm
12 cm
20 cm

The perimeter of the blue line is half the circumference of a circle with a diameter of 12 cm.

$\frac{1}{2}C = \frac{1}{2}\pi d$ so blue perimeter $= \frac{1}{2} \times \pi \times 12$
$= 18.84...$

The two red lines are the same length so the perimeter of the whole shape is $20 + 20 + 18.84... = 58.8$ cm (3 sf)

Any curved lines will mean you have to find part of the circumference of a circle.

As $C = \pi d$ for a whole circle,

for a semicircle $\frac{1}{2}C = \frac{1}{2}\pi d$

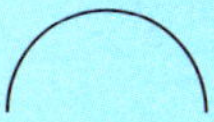

for a quadrant $\frac{1}{4}C = \frac{1}{4}\pi d$

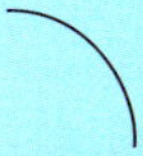

These formulas only find the length of the **curved** part of the lines.

Example
Find the perimeter of this dance floor.

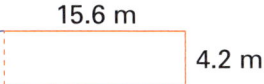

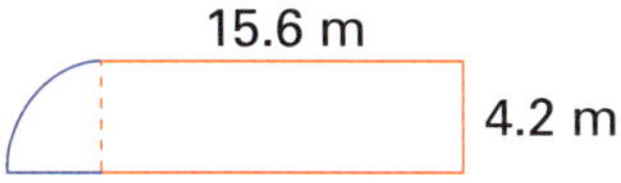

15.6 m
4.2 m

The blue line is part of a quadrant.
It has a radius of 4.2 m, so the diameter is 8.4 m.

The length of the curved blue line is $\frac{1}{4}\pi \times 8.4 = 6.597...$ m
The length of the red lines is $2 \times 15.6 + 4.2 = 35.4$ m
The straight blue line is 4.2 m long.
So the perimeter is $6.597... + 35.4 + 4.2 = 46.2$ m (3 sf)

For shapes like this you will have to add on any straight line lengths to find the perimeter.

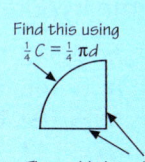

Find this using $\frac{1}{4}C = \frac{1}{4}\pi d$

Then add these lengths on. They are both r, the radius of the circle.

The radius of quadrants or semicircles may not be immediately obvious. If they aren't, look at the other shapes attached to them. The length of the radius or diameter has to be there somewhere! Don't give up!

TEST YOURSELF

1 What is the diameter of a circle with a circumference of:
  a 20 cm   **b** 276 m?

2 What is the radius of a circle with a circumference of:
  a 7 mm   **b** 2.64 km?

3 Find the perimeter of these shapes in metres.
  a   2.3 m
  b   32 cm

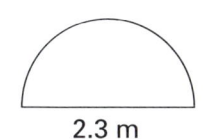

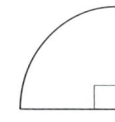

Pythagoras

☐ Pythagoras' theorem

This is for right-angled triangles. It says that:
**The area of the square on the hypotenuse =
the area of the square on the medium side +
the area of the square on the smallest side.**

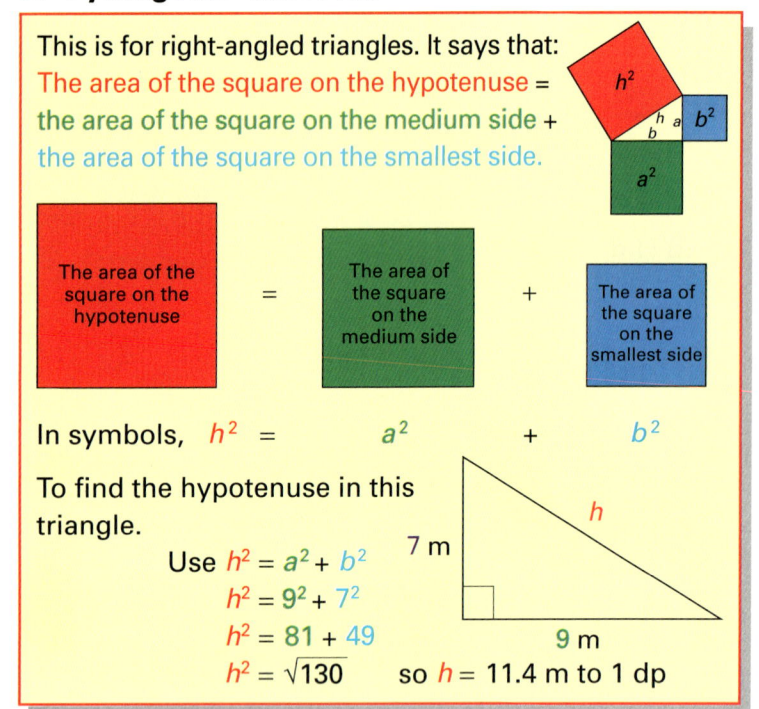

| The area of the square on the hypotenuse | = | The area of the square on the medium side | + | The area of the square on the smallest side |

In symbols, $h^2 = a^2 + b^2$

To find the hypotenuse in this triangle.

Use $h^2 = a^2 + b^2$
$h^2 = 9^2 + 7^2$
$h^2 = 81 + 49$
$h^2 = \sqrt{130}$ so $h = 11.4$ m to 1 dp

Notes

The hypotenuse is the longest side in any right angled triangle. The hypotenuse is always the side opposite the right angle.

$\sqrt{}$ means take the square root of both sides to undo the square.

When you are finding the hypotenuse always make sure that your answer is the longest side!
In this triangle the hypotenuse is the base. Notice that it is still opposite to the right angle.
Make sure you don't round your numbers until the final answer.

Example

a Find h in this triangle.

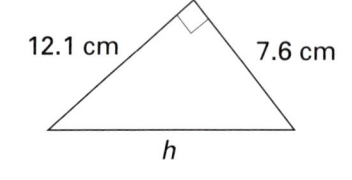

h is the hypotenuse

So $h^2 = 12.1^2 + 7.6^2$
$h^2 = 146.41 + 57.76$
$h^2 = 204.17$
$h = 14.3$ cm (3 sf)

b Find x in this triangle.

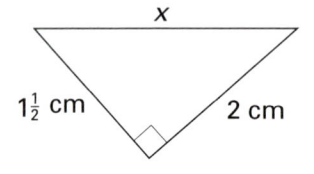

x is the hypotenuse

So $x^2 = (1\frac{1}{2})^2 + 2^2$
$x^2 = \frac{3}{2} \times \frac{3}{2} + 4$
$x^2 = 6\frac{1}{4}$
$x = \sqrt{\frac{25}{4}}$ so $x = \frac{5}{2} = 2\frac{1}{2}$ cm

TEST YOURSELF

1 Find the hypotenuse in each of these triangles.

a h, 17 m, 12 m

b 1.76 m, 2.97 m, h

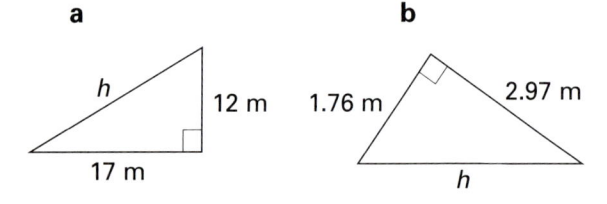

2 Find the length of the missing side in each of these triangles.

a 33 cm, 46 cm

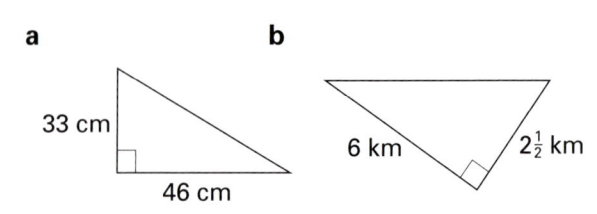

b 6 km, $2\frac{1}{2}$ km

☐ Finding one of the shorter sides

$h^2 = a^2 + b^2$

You rearrange the equation to find the shorter sides.

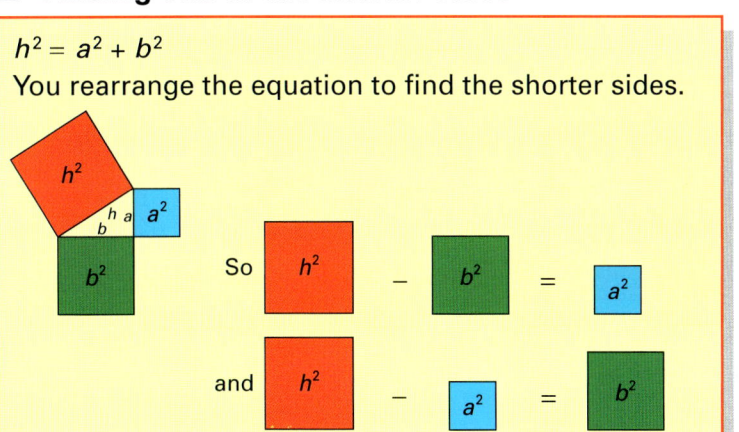

So $h^2 - b^2 = a^2$

and $h^2 - a^2 = b^2$

Example

Find the height of this slide.

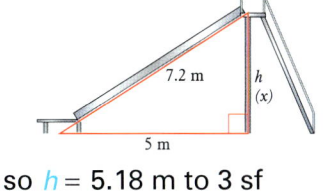

Use $7.2^2 - 5^2 = x^2$
$51.84 - 25 = x^2$
$x^2 = 26.84$
$x = \sqrt{26.84}$ so $h = 5.18$ m to 3 sf

☐ Pythagorean triples

These are where 3 whole numbers work in Pythagoras' theorem, such as $5^2 = 4^2 + 3^2$

See also ➤ **Trigonometry** page 56

☐ Angle in a semicircle

This is the angle you make by joining the diameter to the circumference.
The angle in a semicircle is always 90°.

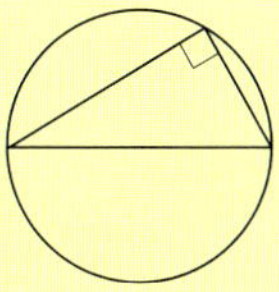

Example

Find the radius of this semicircle.

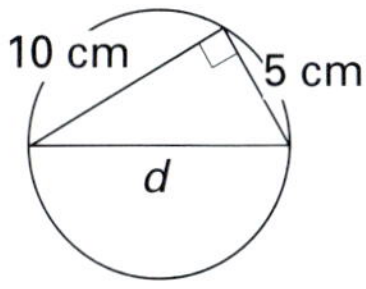

As the triangle is right-angled,
d must be a diameter and $d^2 = 10^2 + 5^2$

so $d^2 = 100 + 25 = 125$
$d = \sqrt{125}$ 11.18... cm

so the radius is 11.18... ÷ 2 = 5.6 cm (1 dp)

Notes

It won't work any other way round will it!

When you get your answer, make sure that the three sides in your triangle make sense.

Check that:

(1) The small side you have found is shorter than the hypotenuse.

(2) The two smaller sides added together are longer than the hypotenuse.

Pythagoras can also be used alongside trigonometry in some problems.

Chapter 18 page 392 ➤

It follows that any triangle in a circle where one of the sides is a diameter must be right-angled.

Don't round your numbers until your final answer.

TEST YOURSELF

1 Find the length of the missing side in each of these triangles.

   a 72 cm, 46 cm

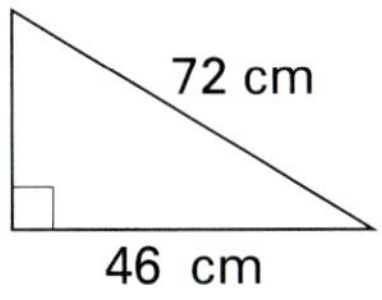

   b 6.5 km, 2.5 km

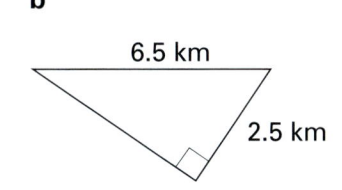

2 Find the lengths of the sides marked with letters.

   a 4 cm, 2 cm, f

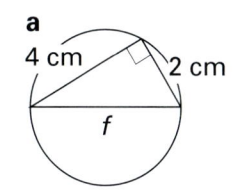

   b r, 6 m, r, 3 m

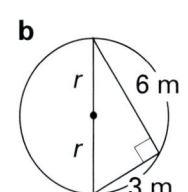

Areas, nets and surface areas

☐ Area by counting

The area of a shape is the space it covers.
If a shape is split into squares you can count its area.
There are 10 whole squares
and 4 half squares here.

So the area is $10 + 4 \times \frac{1}{2} = 12$ cm²

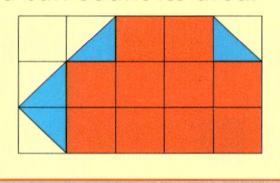

Notes

1 cm / 1 cm The area of this shape is 1 cm²

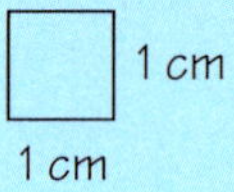

Be careful to tick the areas off in a shape like this to make sure you don't miss any.

☐ Area of a square

The area of a square is length × length

In symbols this is $A = l \times l$ or $A = l^2$

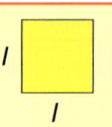

A square is a special rectangle where the length equals the width.
So the area of a square is length × length.

Example

Find the area of this square.
Using $A = l^2$ then $A = 5.6^2$ so $A = 31.36$ cm²

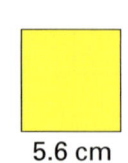

5.6 cm

☐ Area of a rectangle and a triangle

The area of a rectangle is length × width
In symbols, $A = lw$

The area of a triangle is (base × height) ÷ 2
In symbols $A = \frac{1}{2}bh$

The symbols are used as follows:-
Rectangle, l = length, w = width
Triangle, b = base, h = height

Example

Find the area of each of these shapes.

a   2.7 cm / 6.4 cm

b   4 m / 8 m

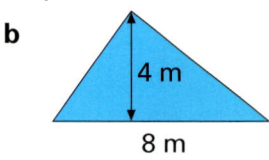

a Area = length × width
   Area = 6.4 × 2.7
   Area = 17.28 cm²

b Area = (base × height) ÷ 2
   Area = (8 × 4) ÷ 2
   Area = 32 ÷ 2 = 16 cm²

Triangles can be shown in different positions. With these, you need to look for a height that is at right angles to the base. In the triangles below, the base is marked **b** and the height is marked **h**.

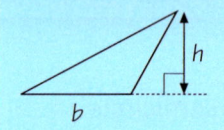

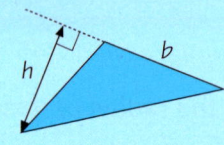

☐ Area of a parallelogram and a kite

The area of a parallelogram is base × height
In symbols, $A = bh$

The area of a kite is $\frac{1}{2} \times$ (diagonals multiplied)
In symbols, $A = \frac{1}{2}xy$

The symbols are used as follows:
Parallelogram, b = base, h = height
Kite, x = diagonal 1, y = diagonal 2

Example

Find the area of each of these shapes.

a   0.24 km / 0.5 km

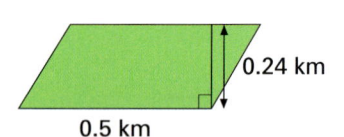

b   5 m / 9.2 m

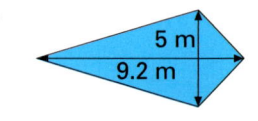

a Area = base × height
   Area = 0.5 × 0.24
   Area = 0.12 km²

b Area = $\frac{1}{2}xy$
   Area = (9.2 × 5) ÷ 2
   Area = 23 m²

Chapter 23 pages 78–89

64

Area of a rhombus and a trapezium

The area of a rhombus is either base × height or $\frac{1}{2}$ × (diagonals multiplied). In symbols, $A = bh$ or $A = \frac{1}{2}xy$

The area of a trapezium is the mean of the parallel sides times the height. In symbols, $A = \frac{1}{2}(a + b)h$

Example

Find the area of each of these shapes

a (rhombus with 4 m and 5.6 m diagonals)

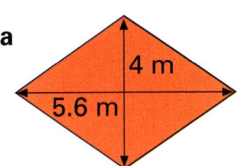

b (trapezium with parallel sides 2.9 mm and 7.7 mm, height 3 mm)

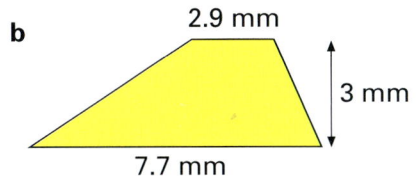

a Area = $\frac{1}{2}xy$
   Area = (5.6 × 4) ÷ 2
   Area = 11.2 m²

b Area = $\frac{1}{2}(a + b)h$
   Area = $\frac{1}{2}$(7.7 + 2.9) × 3
   Area = 15.9 mm²

Area of a circle

The area is the space inside a circle.

If you square the radius, you get a square like this.

You can see that 4 of these squares are too big for the area of a circle.

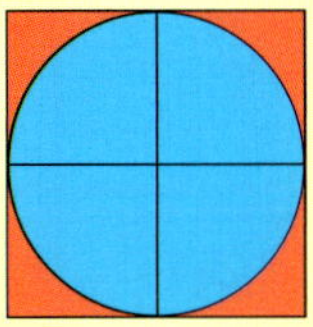

But π times the square of the radius is just right!

So the formula is **Area = π × radius × radius**

Example

Find the area of a circle with a diameter of 10 cm.

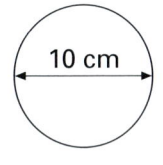

The diameter is 2 × the radius, so the radius is 10 ÷ 2 = 5 cm
Area   = π × radius × radius
So area = π × 5 × 5 = 78.539… = 78.5 cm² (1 dp)

Areas of combined shapes

To find the area of combined shapes:
(1) Split the shape into parts.
(2) Label each part with a letter.
(3) Find any missing lengths.
(4) Work out the separate areas.
(5) Find the total area.

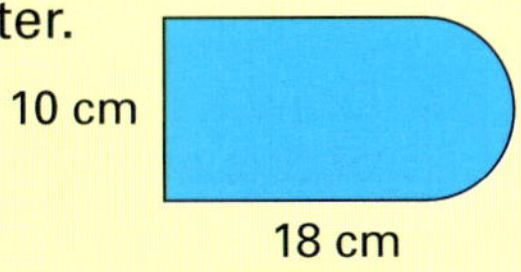

To find the area of this shape, split it into a rectangle and semicircle.

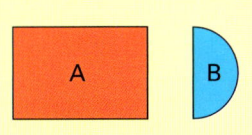

The diameter of the semicircle is 10 cm.
Area A = 10 × 18 = 180 cm²
Area B = $\frac{1}{2}$π × 5² = <u>39.26</u> .. cm²
Total area   = 219.26... cm² = 219 cm² (3 sf)

Notes

A rhombus is a special sort of parallelogram and a special sort of kite. The formula you use for its area depends on which lengths you have got.

The symbols are used as follows:
Rhombus, b = base, h = height,
         x = diagonal 1, y = diagonal 2
Trapezium, a = parallel side 1, b = parallel side 2,
           h = height

You can also work the area of a trapezium out by splitting it into a rectangle and a triangle.

The area is very roughly 3 times the radius squared. You can use this to check that your answer is about right.

You may be asked to find the area of a semicircle.
The best thing to do is find the area of the whole circle and divide it by 2.

This 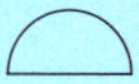   is half of this!

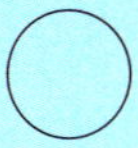

The radius squared is 5 × 5 = 25
So here a rough estimate would be
3 × 25 = 75 cm²

You key in

| π | × | 5 | × | 5 | = |

Always split a combined shape into the least number of shapes you can.

Chapter 23 pages 90–95

☐ Nets

When a solid is opened out and laid flat, the shape that you get is called a net of the solid.

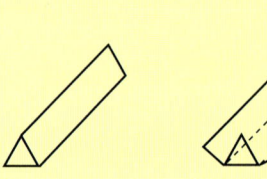

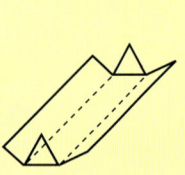

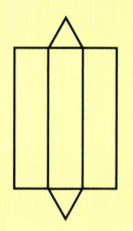

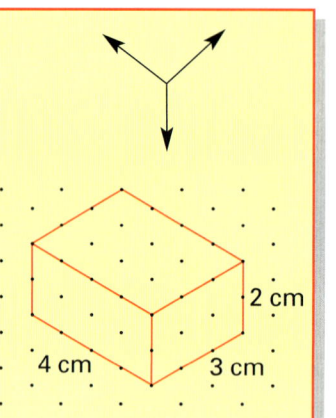

Notes

You don't put flaps on a net unless you're going to make the solid.

Chapter 33 pages 6–98

☐ Drawing

You can also use isometric paper to draw cuboids. Use these 3 directions to draw the edges of the shape. The lengths of the edges of a cuboid are the same when drawn on isometric paper.

This is a cuboid that is 4 cm by 3 cm by 2 cm.

Make sure that the isometric paper is the right way up.

This is right.   This is wrong.

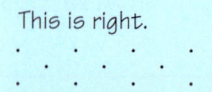

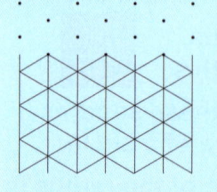

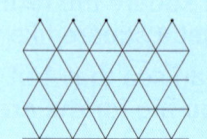

Chapter 30 pages 228–231

TEST YOURSELF

1 Find the area of each of these shapes in m².

a 2.3 m, 1.6 m
b 6.5 m, 3.6 m
c 8.1 m, 4.5 m, 1.7 m
d 3.5 m, 5 m

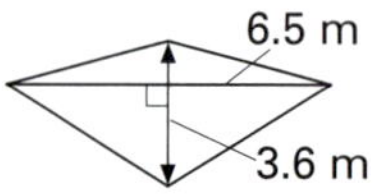

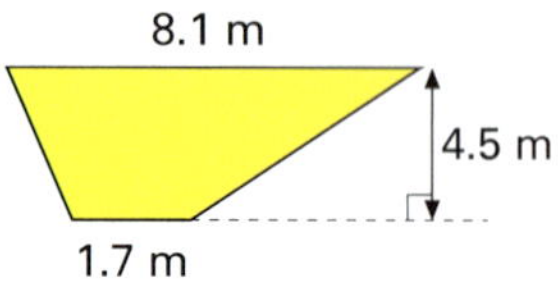

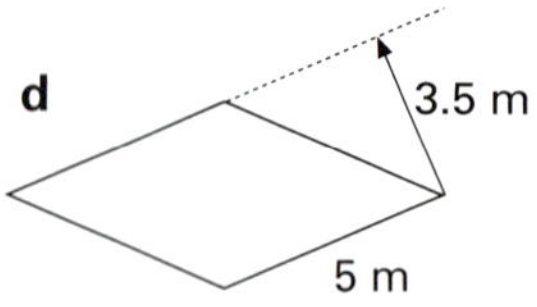

2 Find the area of each of these shapes in m².

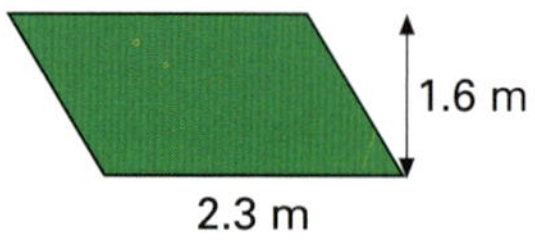

a 9.6 m
b 9 m, 1 m, 6 m, 16 m, 1 m

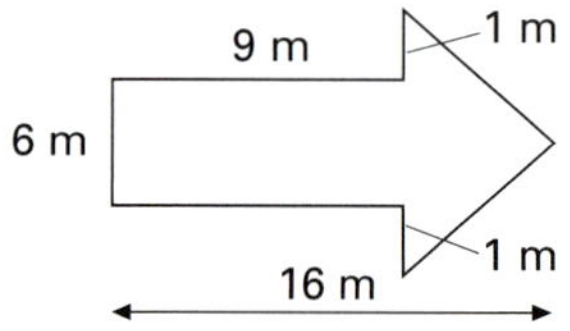

3 Draw a net of each of these solids.
  a Square-based pyramid
  b Cylinder
  c Triangular prism
  d Tetrahedron

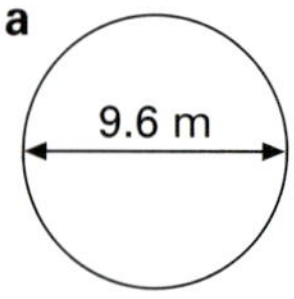

4 Draw a net of this solid.   0.4 cm, 0.6 cm, 1 cm

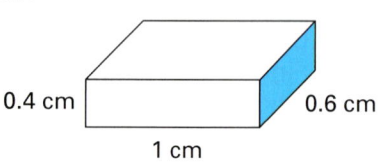

5 Draw this cuboid on isometric paper.   2 cm, 5 cm, 4 cm

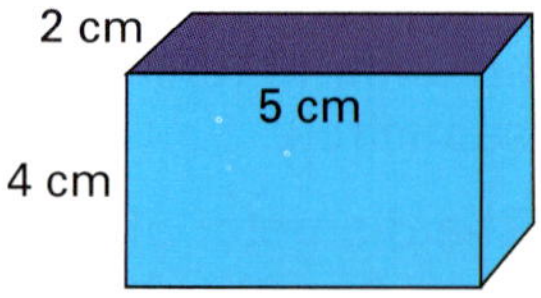

Surface areas of prisms and cylinders

Notes

There are 3 stages to do this:
(1) Sketch the net.
(2) Work out the area of each face on the net.
(3) Find the total area.

Example

Find the surface area of this prism.

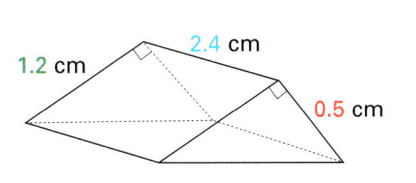

(1) The net

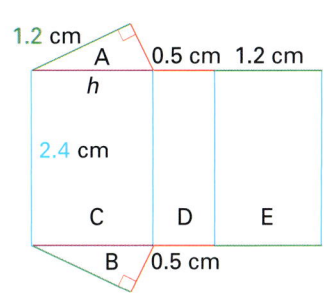

For this prism, right-angled triangles A and B are congruent so they have the same area.

The hypotenuse of triangle A is the width of rectangle C.

You aren't given the hypotenuse, so you have to work it out.

To do this you use Pythagoras:
$h^2 = 1.2^2 + 0.5^2$
$h^2 = 1.69$
so that $h = 1.3$ cm

Chapter 23 pages 99–101

(2) the areas are:
Face A = $\frac{1}{2} \times 1.2 \times 0.5 = 0.3$ cm²
Face B = $\frac{1}{2} \times 1.2 \times 0.5 = 0.3$ cm²
Face C = $\phantom{\frac{1}{2} \times{}} 2.4 \times 1.3 = 3.12$ cm²
Face D = $\phantom{\frac{1}{2} \times{}} 2.4 \times 0.5 = 1.2$ cm²
Face E = $\phantom{\frac{1}{2} \times{}} 2.4 \times 1.2 = 2.88$ cm²

(3) Total area $= 7.8$ cm²

Converting square units

Suppose you have to change cm² to mm².

To understand how to do this it is best to draw two squares.

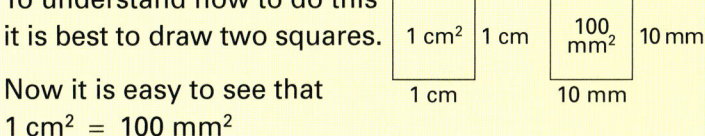

Now it is easy to see that
1 cm² = 100 mm²

This diagram shows you all the conversions for any metric units.

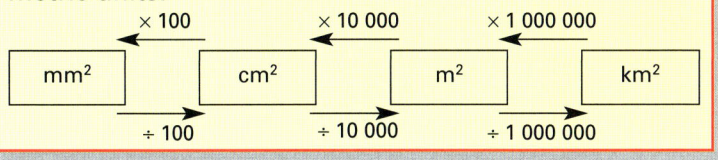

mm² ×100→ cm² ×10 000→ m² ×1 000 000→ km²
mm² ←÷100 cm² ←÷10 000 m² ←÷1 000 000 km²

You can draw pairs of squares like this for other units.
E.g.

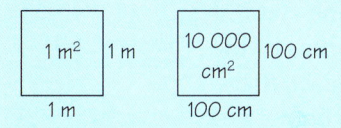

If you are stuck about whether to multiply or divide, use your common sense. For example 20 m² will obviously contain far more than 20 cm². So you will need to multiply by 10 000 to get 20 m² in cm².

TEST YOURSELF

1 Find the surface area of this shape in m².

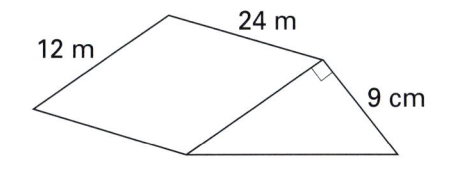

(12 m, 24 m, 9 cm)

2 Change each of these areas into cm².
 a 400 mm²   **b** 8000 mm²   **c** 12 m²

3 Change each of these areas into m².
 a 20 000 cm²   **b** 8 km²   **c** 0.45 km²

67

Angles

☐ **Drawing and measuring**

Angles are measured in degrees. There are 360° in a full turn.

You can use a protractor to measure angles. It has two scales.

It has clockwise scale on the outside and an anticlockwise scale on the inside.

It also has a cross and a zero line.

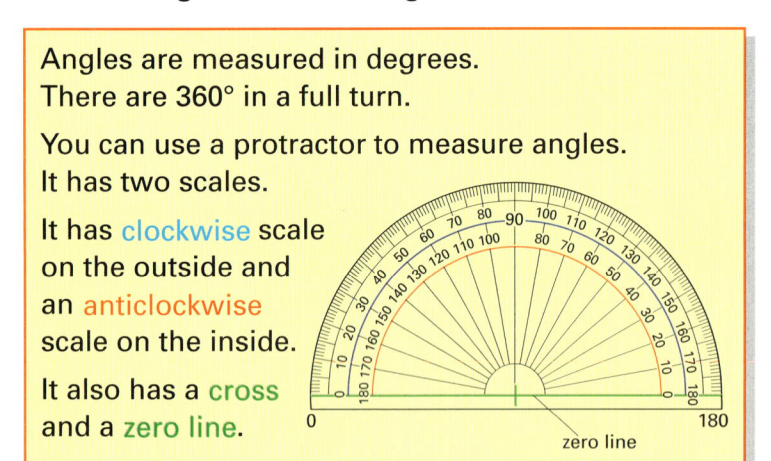

Make sure that one side of the angle is on the zero line of the protractor. Read the angle on the scale that starts at zero.

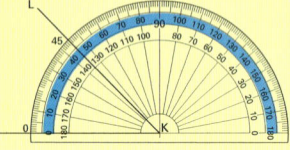

Use the blue scale. The angle JKL is 45°.

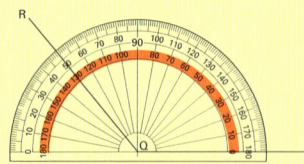

Use the red scale. The angle PQR is 130°.

To draw an angle of 60° at P.

(1) Draw a horizontal line.
(2) Put a small × at P.
(3) Put the cross of the protractor on the ×. The zero line of the protractor must lie on the horizontal line.
(4) Find 60° on the clockwise scale.
(5) Make a mark at this point.
(6) Join the × to this mark with a straight line.
(7) Label the angle 60°.

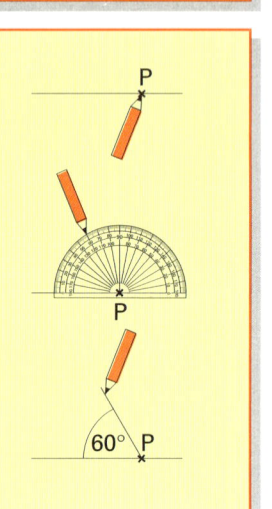

Notes

Remember that this direction is clockwise.

...this is the way that the hands on a clock move...

and this direction is anticlockwise

...this is the opposite way.

Always make sure that you read the scale that starts at zero.

Also think about the size of the angle. An acute angle must be less than 90°.

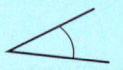

An obtuse angle must be between 90° and 180°.

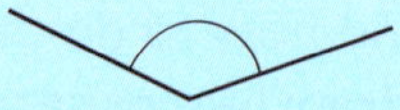

A reflex angle must be bigger than 180°.

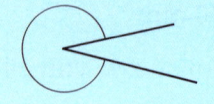

Chapter 26 pages 144–145

TEST YOURSELF

1 Use the diagram to find the size of these angles.
   a AP̂B   **c** AP̂D   **e** ZP̂B   **g** ZP̂D
   b AP̂C   **d** AP̂E   **f** ZP̂C   **h** ZP̂E

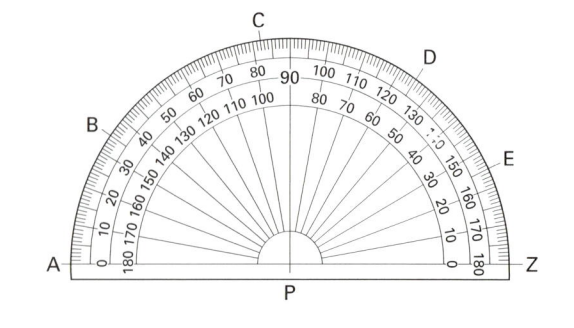

2 Draw these angles:
   a 45°   **c** 120°   **e** 105°   **g** 270°
   b 78°   **d** 143°   **f** 171°   **h** 230°

68

☐ Angles on a straight line

Angles on a straight line add up to 180°.

$a = 180° - 65°$
$= 115°$

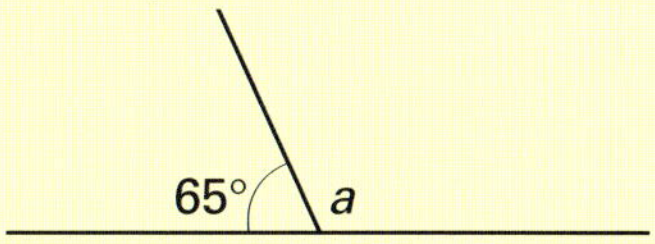

☐ Angles round a point

Angles round a point add up to 360°.

$b = 360° - 125°$
$= 235°$

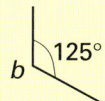

☐ Angles in a triangle

Angles in a triangle add up to 180°.

$52° + 37° = 89°$
$c = 180° - 89°$
$= 91°$

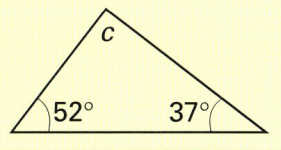

☐ Angles in a quadrilateral

Angles in a quadrilateral add up to 360°.

$36° + 56° + 122° = 214°$
$d = 360° - 214°$
$= 146°$

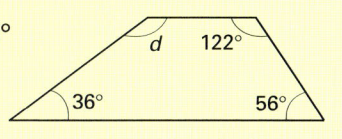

☐ Opposite angles

Angles that are opposite each other in a cross are equal.
g is opposite the 57°
so $g = 57°$.
$e = 180° - 57° = 123°$.
$f = e = 123°$.

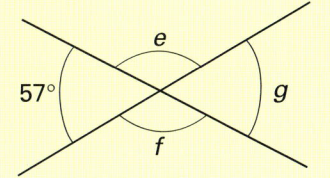

Notes

Learn these important results and how to work out angles like this.

You won't be able to measure angles in questions that want you to use these results.

Add up the angles you know.
Take the total away from 180°.

Add up the angles you know.
Take the total away from 360°.

These are sometimes called vertically opposite angles.

The angle e is on a straight line with the 57° angle.
e and f are opposite angles.

Chapter 26 pages 146–150

TEST YOURSELF

1 Calculate the angles marked with letters

a 81°, a

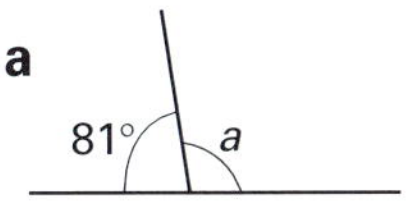

b 160°, 123°, b

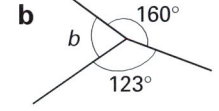

c 93°, 64°, c

d d, 100°, 95°, 80°

e 72°, f, e, g

f 70°, h, h

g 81°, i (with two right angles)

h 30°, j, k, 130°

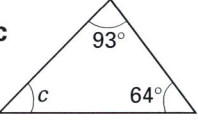

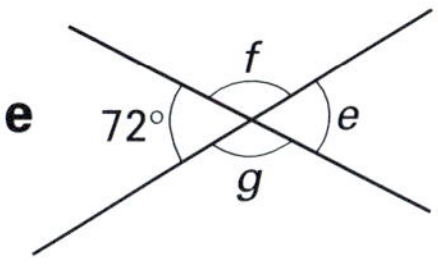

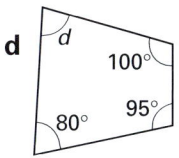

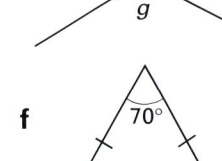

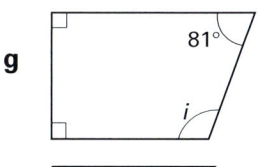

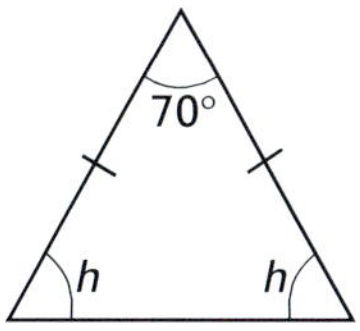

69

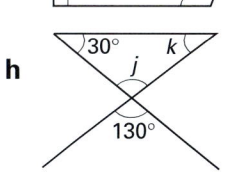

☐ Angles in parallel lines

You should know these angle facts when working with parallel lines.

Corresponding angles are equal
so $a = p$, $b = q$,
$c = r$ and $d = s$.

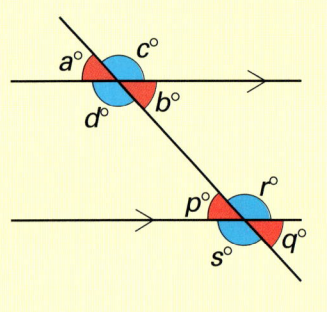

Alternate angles are equal
so $b = p$ and
$d = r$.

Notes

You can also use opposite angles and angles on a straight line to work out the angles in parallel lines.

In some questions you may have a choice about which angle facts to use. In this situation it doesn't matter which you choose to use.

☐ Angles in polygons

An **interior angle** is an angle inside a shape where two sides meet.

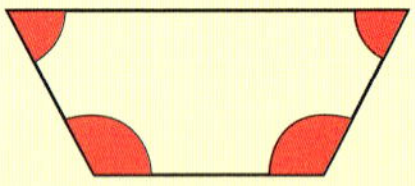

An **exterior angle** is an angle outside a shape where two sides meet.

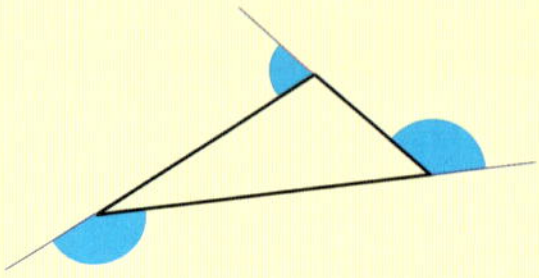

The exterior angles of a polygon add up to 360°.

If a polygon is regular all of the exterior angles are the same.

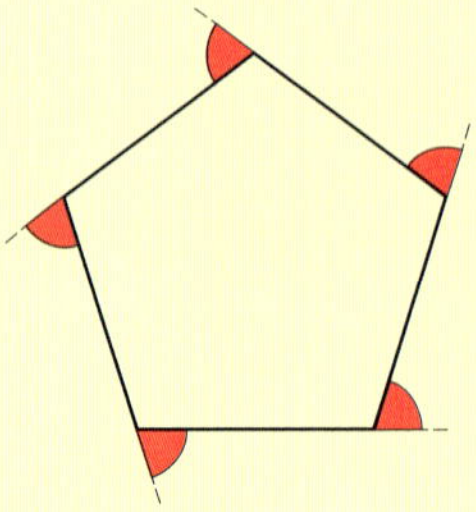

For this regular pentagon,

exterior angle = $\frac{360}{5}$ = 72°

The interior angle + the exterior angle = 180°.
So interior angle = 180° – exterior angle.

For this regular hexagon,

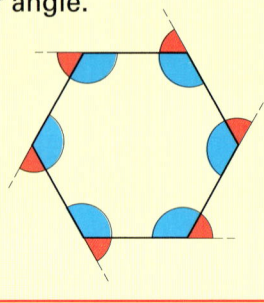

exterior angle = $\frac{360}{6}$ = 60°

interior angle = 180° – 60°
= 120°

The red angles are all interior angles.

The blue angles are all exterior angles.
An exterior angle is not the whole angle outside a shape.
You need to make one side longer and look at the angle between this new line and the next side.

A polygon is any shape with straight sides.

This is because of angles on a straight line.

A corner of a polygon is called a **vertex**.

☐ Angles in circles

You should learn these three angle facts.

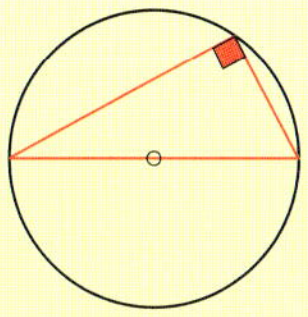

1. The angle in a **semicircle** is **90°**.

   > See also **Pythagoras** page 13

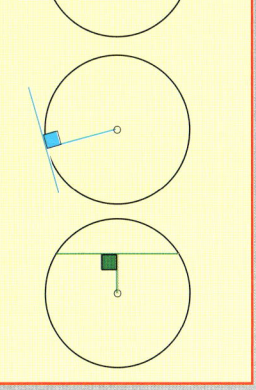

2. A **radius** meets a **tangent** at **90°**.

3. A **line from the centre** of a circle to the **midpoint of a chord** meets it at **90°**.

Notes

A chord is a straight line from one point to another on the circumference of a circle. It does not go through the centre.

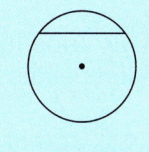

A tangent is a straight line that just touches the circle.

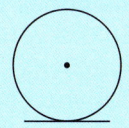

☐ Angles in circles

The bearing of D from C means you are at C.

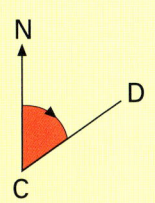

The bearing of C from D means you are at D.

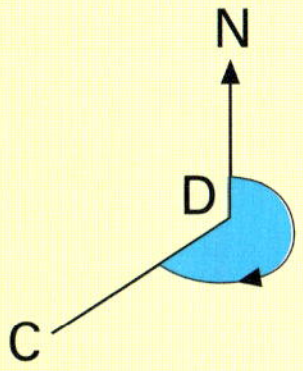

Face North. Turn clockwise until you face D.

Face North. Turn clockwise until you face C.

To do a scale drawing:
(1) Do a sketch first.
(2) Use a sensible scale.
(3) Draw as accurately as possible.

A bearing has 3 figures.

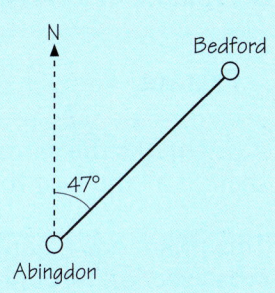

The angle you turn through is the bearing. The bearing of Bedford from Abingdon is 047°.

Chapter 26 pages 152–161

TEST YOURSELF

1 Calculate the angles marked with letters. Give reasons for your answers.

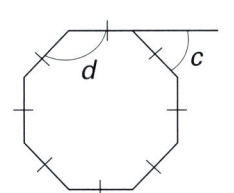

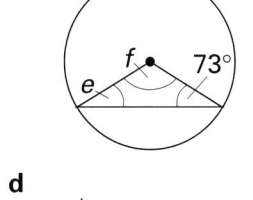

a 73°, a, b

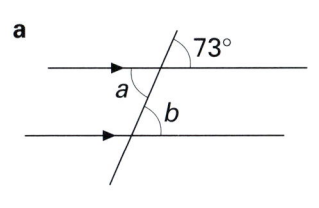

b octagon with angles c, d

c circle with angles e, f, 73°

d 62°, g, h, i

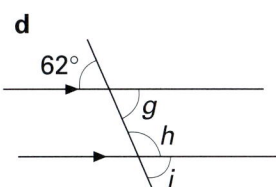

2 a Measure the bearing of B from A.
  b Work out the bearing of A from B.

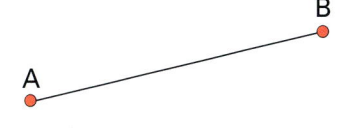

3 A ferry travels from point F, 20 km on a bearing 065° to G. It then travels 25 km on a bearing of 135° to H. Use a scale drawing to find:
  a the distance of H from F
  b the bearing of H from F.

Volume

☐ Volume and capacity

Volume is the amount of space a solid takes up.
Capacity is the amount of space in a hollow object.

This cube has a volume of 1 cm³.
All its sides are 1 cm long.

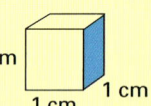

Look at this shape. If you count the cubes there are 12.
So the volume is 12 cm³.

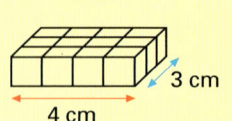

But you can also do length × width = 4 × 3 = 12 cm³.

This shape is similar, but there are 2 layers. The volume is the number in a layer × height. The volume is 4 × 3 × 2 = 24 cm³

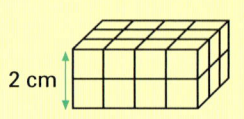

So **volume of a cuboid** = length × width × height

☐ Prisms

A prism has the same cross section all the way through.

This prism has a pentagonal cross section throughout its length.

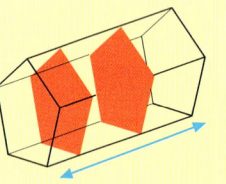

Volume of a prism = Area of cross section × length

Example

Find the volume of this triangular prism.

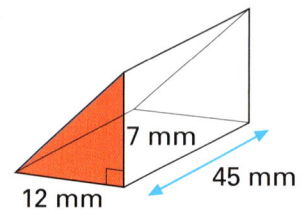

Area of cross section
= $\frac{1}{2}$ × 12 × 7 = 42 mm²

Volume of prism
= 42 × 45 = 1890 mm³

☐ Cylinders

Like a prism,

Volume = Area of cross section × height

so Volume = $\pi r^2 h$ where r is the radius.

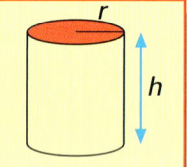

Example

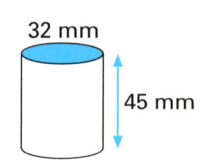

Find the volume of this cylinder.

Using $V = \pi r^2 h$ and $r = 32 ÷ 2 = 16$ mm

$V = \pi \times 16^2 \times 45$

$V = 36\,191.14$ so $V = 36\,200$ mm³ = 36.2 cm³ (3 sf)

72

Notes

A mountain has volume.
A fuel tank has capacity.
A cube with all its sides 1 m long has a volume of 1 m³.

If a cube like this is hollow and filled with water, it has a capacity of 1 ml.

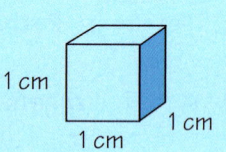

A cube is a special sort of cuboid.
All its lengths are the same.
You can write:

Volume of a cube = length × length × length

or Volume of a cube = (length)³

You need to revise area formulas.

Square: $A = l^2$ l = length
Rectangle: $A = lw$ l = length, w = width
Triangle: $A = \frac{1}{2}bh$ b = base, h = height
Circle: $A = \pi r^2$ r = radius

Kites, parallelograms and rhombuses can be worked out by splitting them into two triangles. You are normally given the formula for the area of a trapezium.

Sometimes you may not be given the height or base of the triangle. Then you may have to use Pythagoras' theorem or trigonometry to work it out.

Chapter 30 pages 239–251

Strictly, a cylinder isn't a prism as a circle is not a polygon.
When using the formula for volume the length of a cylinder is usually referred to as the height.

This is a cubic centimetre.
It has 10 × 10 × 10 mm³ in it.
So 1000 mm³ = 1 cm³.

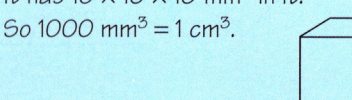

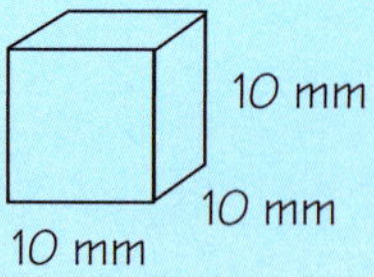

☐ Volumes of compound shapes

To find the volume of combined shapes:

(1) Split the shape into parts.
(2) Label each part with a letter.
(3) Find any missing lengths.
(4) Work out the separate areas.
(5) Find the total cross-sectional area.
(6) Multiply this total by the length.

To find the volume of this shape, split the cross section into a rectangle and a triangle.

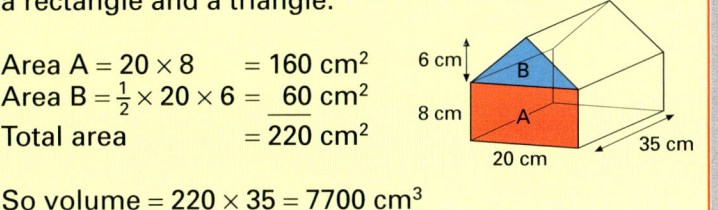

Area A = 20 × 8 = 160 cm²
Area B = ½ × 20 × 6 = 60 cm²
Total area = 220 cm²

So volume = 220 × 35 = 7700 cm³

Notes

Always split a combined shape into the least number of shapes you can.

Chapter 30 pages 252–256

☐ Density

You can show the formula

Density = Mass/Volume in a triangle

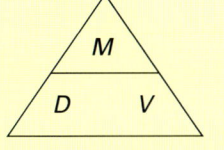

You can then use the triangle to find

Mass = Density × Volume and Volume = Mass/Density

As you read the triangle from left to right it is in alphabetical order.

If you cover up one of the letters with your finger you can see what to do.

So if you cover up M then you are left with DV. This means M = D × V

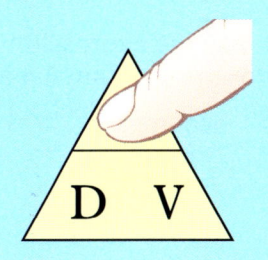

Example

Find the mass of this block if the density is 1.6 g/cm³

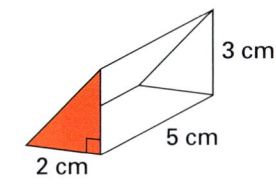

Mass = Density × Volume

The volume is ½ × (2 × 3) × 5 = 15 cm³
So Mass = 1.6 × 15 = 24 g

TEST YOURSELF

1 Find the volume of these shapes. Round your answers to 2 decimal places.

a) 6.4 cm, 6.4 cm, 6.4 cm

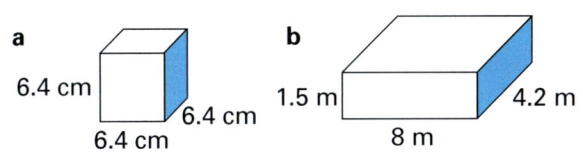

b) 1.5 m, 8 m, 4.2 m

2 Find the volume of each of these solids.

a) 1.8 m, 1.4 m, 4.2 m

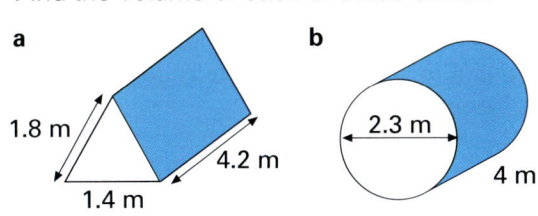

b) 2.3 m, 4 m

3 Find the volume of this shape.
4.1 m, 2.1 m, 2.4 m, 0.9 m, 0.8 m, 3.6 m

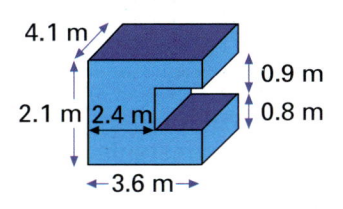

4 A shape has a mass of 220 g and a density of 5.5 g/cm³. What is its volume?

5 The mass of some gel is 21 kg. Its volume is 14 litres. Find its density in kg/m³.
(1 m³ = 1000 litres)

Dimensional analysis

☐ Cylinders

> The dimension of a formula is the number of lengths that are multiplied together. Lengths are variables.
>
> Although the lengths in formulas often have different symbols, it is best if you call them all L.
>
> A constant is just a number like π, 2, 3.8, $12\frac{1}{2}$, 0.2 etc. Constants cannot take different values. Call these C.
>
> To find the dimension of a formula you can ignore constants.
>
> An expression for length will come out with dimension L.
>
> An expression for area will come out with dimension L^2.
>
> An expression for volume will come out with dimension L^3.

Notes

A formula has an equals sign in it. An expression does not have an equals sign in it.

A variable can take different values. For example the height of this triangle h, can be any value you decide to give it.

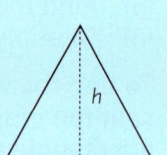

Example

Write down the dimensions of these expressions.
b, h and r are all lengths. **a** $\frac{1}{2}bh$ **b** $\pi r^2 h$ **c** $\frac{0.4\,bh}{r}$

a Put in C for the constant $\frac{1}{2}$ and L for b and L for h, so $\frac{1}{2}bh$ becomes $C \times L \times L$.
Now ignore C. $L \times L = L^2$, so the expression is for area.

b Put in C for π and L for r and L for h, so $\pi r^2 h$ becomes $C \times L^2 \times L$.
Now ignore C.
$L^2 \times L = L^3$, so the expression is for volume.

c Put in C for the constant 0.4 and L for b, h, and r so $\frac{0.4\,bh}{r}$ becomes $\frac{C \times L \times L}{L}$.

Now ignore C. $(L \times L) \div L = L^2 \div L = L$

So the expression is for length.

You may get something such as L^4, L^5 or higher L^0, L^{-1}, L^{-2} or lower. In these cases you do not have an expression or formula that represents length, area or volume.

π is a constant at 3.141.... It cannot take any other value.

Notice that area × length = volume. (This is the type of dimensional multiplying you do to find the volume of a prism.)

Notice that area ÷ length = length. (This is the type of dimensional dividing you do to find the length of a rectangle if you are given its width and area.)

☐ More than one term

> Some formulas have more than one term e.g. $2\pi r^2 + 2\pi rh$. In these all the terms must have the same dimension to be a formula for length, area or volume.

Chapter 30 pages 257–259

Example

Write down the dimensions of the formula $D = 8\pi r^2 + 8\pi rh$.
Replacing constants and variables, $D = C^2 \times L^2 + C^2 \times L \times L$
Ignoring the C^2 terms, $D = L^2 + L^2$, giving an area as well.

TEST YOURSELF

In these questions, f, j and m are used for units of length, a and b are constants. Write down the dimensions of the formulas.

1 a $F = 2\pi m$ **b** $G = fjm$ **c** $H = 4\pi m^2$
   d $S = 0.2\pi fm^2$ **e** $T = \dfrac{j^2 m}{3\pi f}$

2 Write down, with reasons, which one of these expressions is not a length, area or volume.

   a $fj^2 + \pi m^2$ **b** $\dfrac{3\pi f m^2}{10^7 j^2}$ **c** $\dfrac{\pi j^2 m^3}{7 f^2}$

Symmetry

☐ Lines of symmetry

A line of symmetry divides a shape into two identical halves.
Each part is a reflection of the other.
If you fold a shape along a line of symmetry the two parts will fit exactly on top of each other.

This shape has two lines of symmetry.
The lines of symmetry are shown by the red dashed lines.

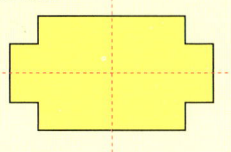

☐ Rotational symmetry

The order of rotational symmetry of a shape is the number of times that the shape looks the same as it makes a full turn.

Examples

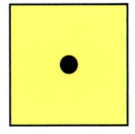

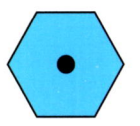

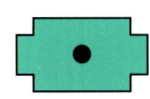

order 4   order 6   order 2   order 1

Regular polygons have both rotational and line symmetry.
This regular hexagon has rotational symmetry order 6 and 6 lines of symmetry.

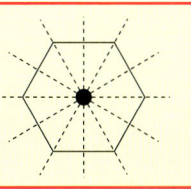

☐ Symmetry in 3D

3D shapes may have symmetry.

If so they have planes of symmetry.

Here are the planes of symmetry for this prism.

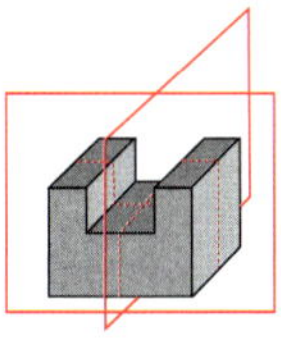

Notes

A line of symmetry is sometimes called a mirror line.
Some other examples are

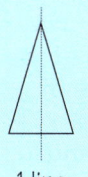

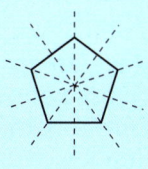

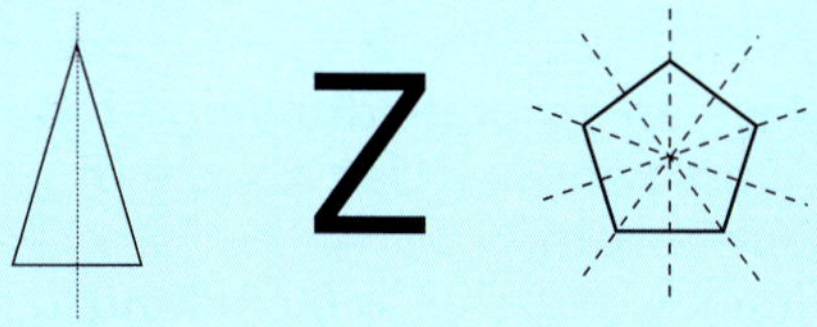

1 line   no lines   5 lines

A line of symmetry is always drawn as a dashed line.

You are allowed to ask for tracing paper in your exam.
You can use tracing paper to find the order of rotational symmetry.
- Trace the shape and the centre of rotation.
- Hold the centre still with a pencil.
- Rotate the tracing paper and count how many times the shape looks the same as you make one complete turn.

The number of sides in a regular polygon tells you the number of lines of symmetry and the order of rotational symmetry.

Chapter 32 pages 284–292

TEST YOURSELF

1. Copy these shapes. For each shape:
   a draw all the lines of symmetry
   b write down the order of rotational symmetry.

   A   B   C
   D    E   F

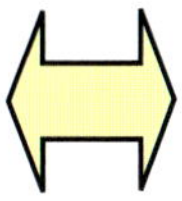

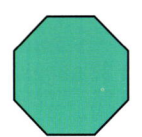

2. Copy this diagram. Draw the reflection of triangle ABC in the dashed mirror line.

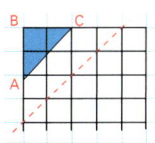

3. Copy these shapes. Draw all the planes of symmetry. Use a separate diagram for each.

   A Equilateral triangular prism
   B Square based pyramid

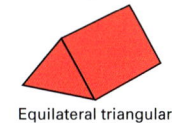

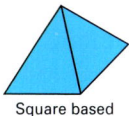

75

Loci

☐ Constructing triangles

> How you draw a triangle depends on the data you are given.

Examples

a Make an accurate drawing of the triangle shown. Use a scale of 1 cm to 1 m. 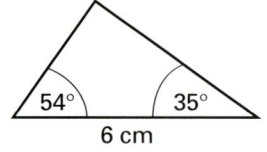
First draw the base 6 cm long.
Next use a protractor to measure the angles.
Finally make the sides longer until they cross.

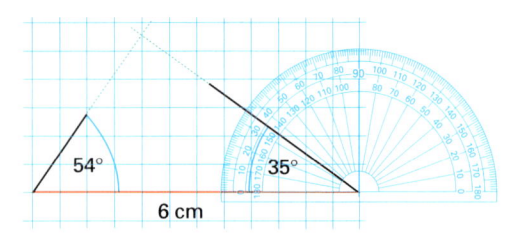

b Draw a triangle with sides 5 cm, 4 cm and 2 cm.
Draw the base 5 cm long.
Draw an arc radius 4 cm from A.
Draw an arc radius 2 cm from B. Make sure it crosses the first arc.
Join A and B to where the arcs cross.

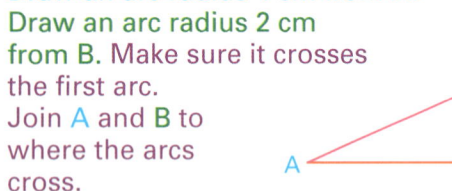

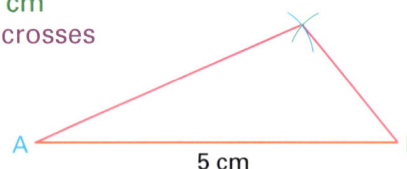

☐ Constructing an angle bisector

> Put your compass point on A.
> Draw an arc through both lines to mark B and C.
> Then, keeping your compasses open at the same length:
> - Put your compass point on B.
> - Draw an arc.
> - Put your compass point on C.
> - Draw an arc to meet the first one. Call this D. Join A to D.

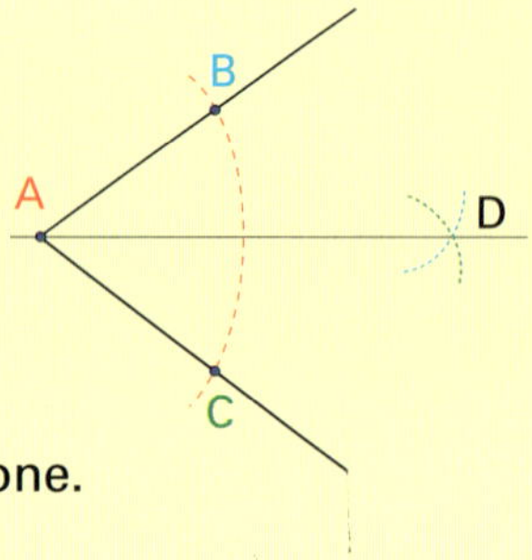

☐ Constructing a perpendicular bisector

> To construct the perpendicular bisector of EF.
> Put your compass point on E.
> Draw arcs above and below the line.
> Then, keeping your compasses open at the same length:
> - Put your compass point on F.
> - Draw arcs to meet the first two at points G and H.
> - Now join G to H.

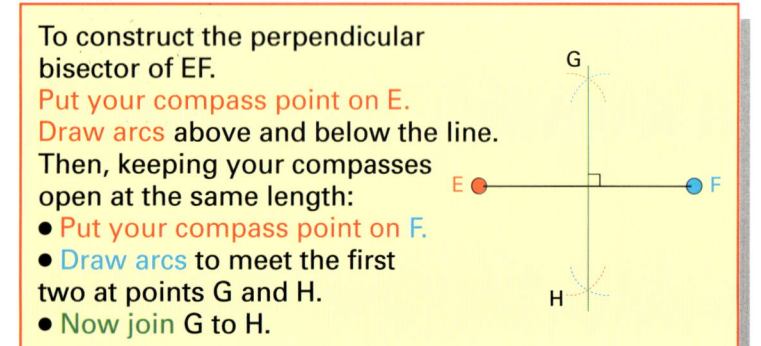

Notes

Questions on drawing triangles always give you at least one side. This is because you cannot draw **one** triangle if you are just given angles.

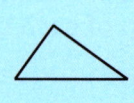

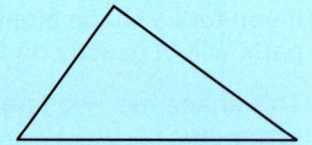

These two triangles have the same angles but they are different sizes.

Do the drawing in the order of the colours, red, blue then green.

It is best to use the longest side as a base.

Do the drawing in the order of the colours red, blue, green then purple.

You will need to have your compasses open to a reasonable width to start with. About 3 or 4 cm is usually enough.

Accuracy is *essential* with diagrams like this. You are normally only allowed errors of around 1 or 2 mm.

Perpendicular means at right angles. Bisection is when you cut something in half. So the perpendicular bisector of a line is at right angles to the line *and* cuts the line into two equal parts.

Chapter 33 pages 308–315

☐ Loci

There are four main types of loci.
(1) **Fixed distance** from **a fixed point**. The locus is **a circle**.

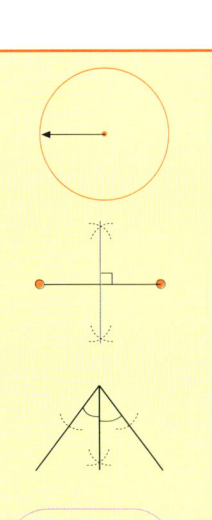

(2) **The same distance** from **two fixed points**. The locus is the **perpendicular bisector of the line between the two points**.

(3) **The same distance** from **two fixed lines**. The locus is the **angle bisector of the two lines**.

(4) **Fixed distance** from **a fixed line**. The locus is in the shape of **a running track**.

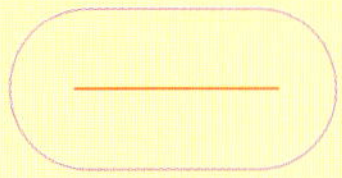

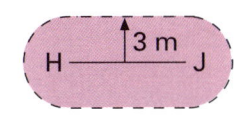

Notes

To draw loci you need to make sure you can do basic constructions. In particular you should be able to draw:

a perpendicular bisector
an angle bisector.

It could help you to remember these loci if you put them all together to make a model sailor!

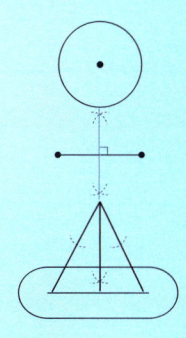

Examples

Draw the loci of:
a a point on the rim of a wheel 35 cm from the centre A
b a ship always the same distance from two buoys B and C
c a pole DG in a ridge tent so that it is always equidistant from the two walls of the tent ED and DF
d a goat tethered so it is always less than 3 m from a rail HJ.

In part **d** shade the region where the goat can graze.

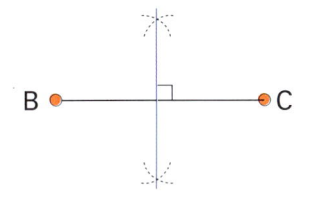

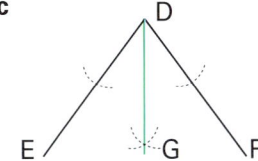

A region is where an object can be anything up to a given distance away.

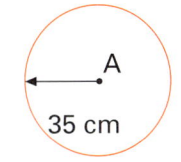

To show something which is always less than a given distance you need to use a broken line on the edge of a region.

Chapter 33 pages 316–326 ➔

TEST YOURSELF

1 Draw a triangle with sides 6 cm, 5 cm and 3 cm. Measure the angles in the triangle.

2 A mobile phone mast is to be situated so that it is equidistant from two motorways. It must also be between 2 km and 4 km from the centre of a housing estate (shown by the red shaded area). Copy the diagram and show where the mast may be positioned.

Scale 1 cm = 2 km

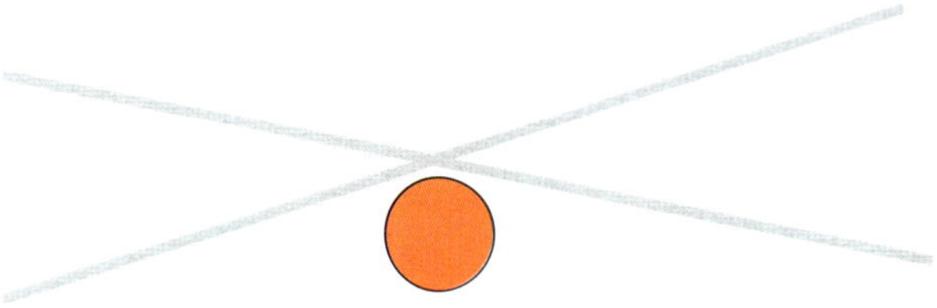

Practice questions

1 The diagram shows shapes Q and R which are transformations of shape P.

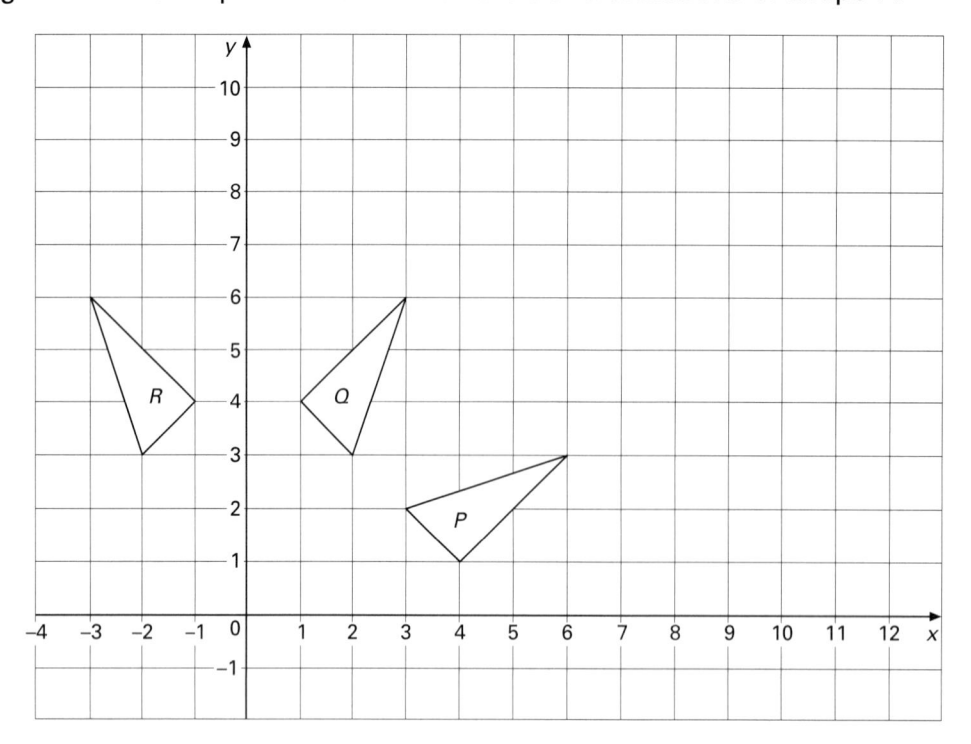

    a Describe fully the **single** transformation which takes P onto R. (3)

    b Describe fully the **single** transformation which takes P onto Q. (2)

    c Copy the diagram and draw an enlargement of shape P with scale factor 2, centre (3, 2) (2)

SEG, 1999, Paper 13

2

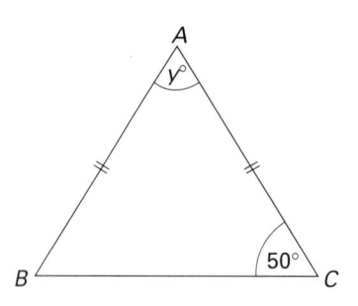

Diagram **NOT** accurately drawn

In triangle ABC, AB = AC and angle C = 50°.

    a Write down the special name for triangle ABC. (1)

    b Work out the value of y. (2)

Edexcel, 1999, Paper 4

4 Handling data

- [ ] **Dealing with data**
- [ ] **Averages**
- [ ] **Comparing data**
- [ ] **Simple probability**
- [ ] **Laws of probability**
- [ ] **Tree diagrams**

Practice questions

Dealing with data

☐ Bar-charts, pie-charts and pictograms

Bar-charts, pie-charts and pictograms are all different types of diagrams which you can use to help you understand data.

This bar-chart shows the number of students who watched a particular TV channel.

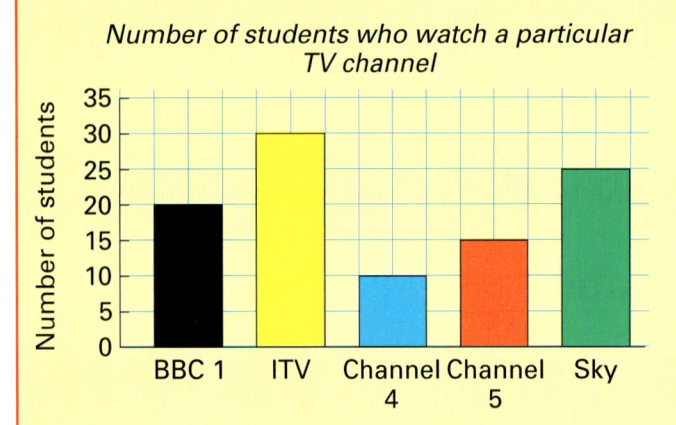

Number of students who watch a particular TV channel

ITV was the most popular channel with 30 students watching it. The least popular channel was Channel 4. Only 10 students watched that channel.

You could show the data on the bar chart with this pictogram.

BBC 1   ☐ ☐

ITV   ☐ ☐ ☐

Channel 4 ☐

Channel 5 ☐ ☐

Sky   ☐ ☐ ☐

Key: ☐ = 10 people

☐ Pie-charts

A **pie-chart** shows how something has been divided up. The angle of each sector represents the number of items.

Example

The table gives the colours of cars in a car park.
Draw a pie-chart to show this data.

Black	Blue	Green	Red	Silver	White
21	18	13	20	8	10

Notes

A bar-chart has a space between the bars.

Remember to read the scale on the axis.

There were 25 students who watched either Channel 4 or Channel 5.

The modal channel is ITV, as that was the most popular channel.

Check how many people, or objects, each picture represents.

In this example you use ☐ to represent 10 people and ☐ represents 5 people.

Always give a pictogram a key.

There are 90 cars altogether.
The angles at the centre of the circle add to 360°.
So each car is represented by 360 ÷ 90 = 4°.

Working out the angles for each sector gives:

Colour	Angles
Black	21 × 4° = 84°
Blue	18 × 4° = 72°
Green	13 × 4° = 52°
Red	20 × 4° = 80°
Silver	8 × 4° = 32°
White	10 × 4° = 40°

(1) Draw a circle and mark the centre. Draw a line from the centre to the top of the circle.
(2) Draw the first angle of 84°.
(3) Measure the next angle (72°) from the line you have just drawn.
(4) Carry on until you have drawn all the angles.

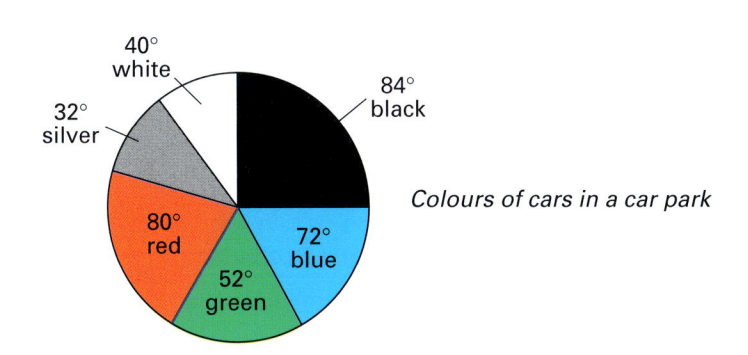

Colours of cars in a car park

Notes

Adding up,
21 + 18 + 13 + 20 + 8 + 10 = 90

If there were 180 cars, each car would be shown by 360 ÷ 180 = 2°

If there were 120 cars, each car would be shown by 360 ÷ 120 = 3°

Check that your angles add up to 360°.

Label each sector and don't forget a title.

Chapter 3 pages 50–54

TEST YOURSELF

1 The mathematics GCSE results at Riverdean School last year were:

Grade	A*	A	B	C	D	E	F	G
%	2	6	24	22	21	15	7	3

  a Draw a bar-chart to show this information.
  b What percentage of students gained grades A* to C?
  c What was the modal grade?

2 Draw a pictogram to show how Steven spends his money each week.

Spending	rent	food	clothes	bus	other
Amount	£65	£50	£20	£15	£30

3 Draw a pie-chart to show the data in question **2**.

4 A survey to find out how pupils travelled to school produced the following results. Draw a pie-chart to show this data.

Method of travel	walk	cycle	bus	car
Number of pupils	250	50	270	150

81

☐ Scatter graphs

> A **scatter graph** is a diagram that is used to see if there is any connection, or correlation, between two sets of data.

Notes

Correlation is a measure of how strongly two sets of data are connected.

Example

Here are the test scores for a group of students taking French and German.

| French | 45 | 56 | 58 | 63 | 74 | 58 | 62 | 42 | 39 | 45 |
| German | 50 | 58 | 56 | 62 | 76 | 53 | 63 | 46 | 35 | 43 |

Find the likely German test score for a student who was absent for the German test but who scored 48 on the French test.

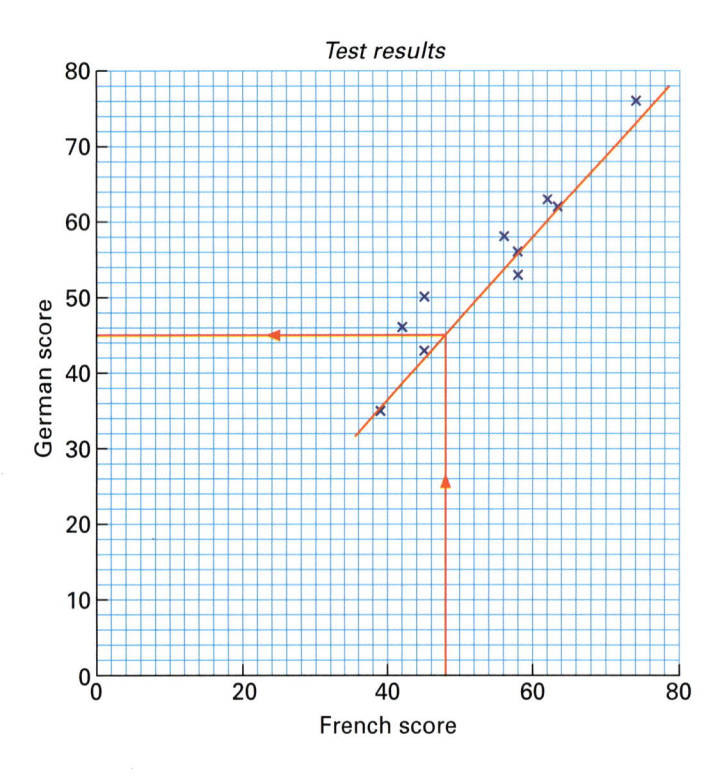

Put one value on the x axis and the other value on the y axis. Usually it does not matter which way round they go.

You can use scatter graphs to estimate missing values.
First draw the line of best fit.
You can use this line to estimate data values. Go up to the line and across or across to the line and down. You must show the lines you have used to read off values.

The points on this graph lie roughly in a straight line. This line is called the **line of best fit**. It goes through the middle of the points.

First find the score of 48 on the French axis. Then draw a line up to meet the line of best fit. Finally draw a horizontal line to the German axis and read off the value.

The estimate for the German mark is 45.

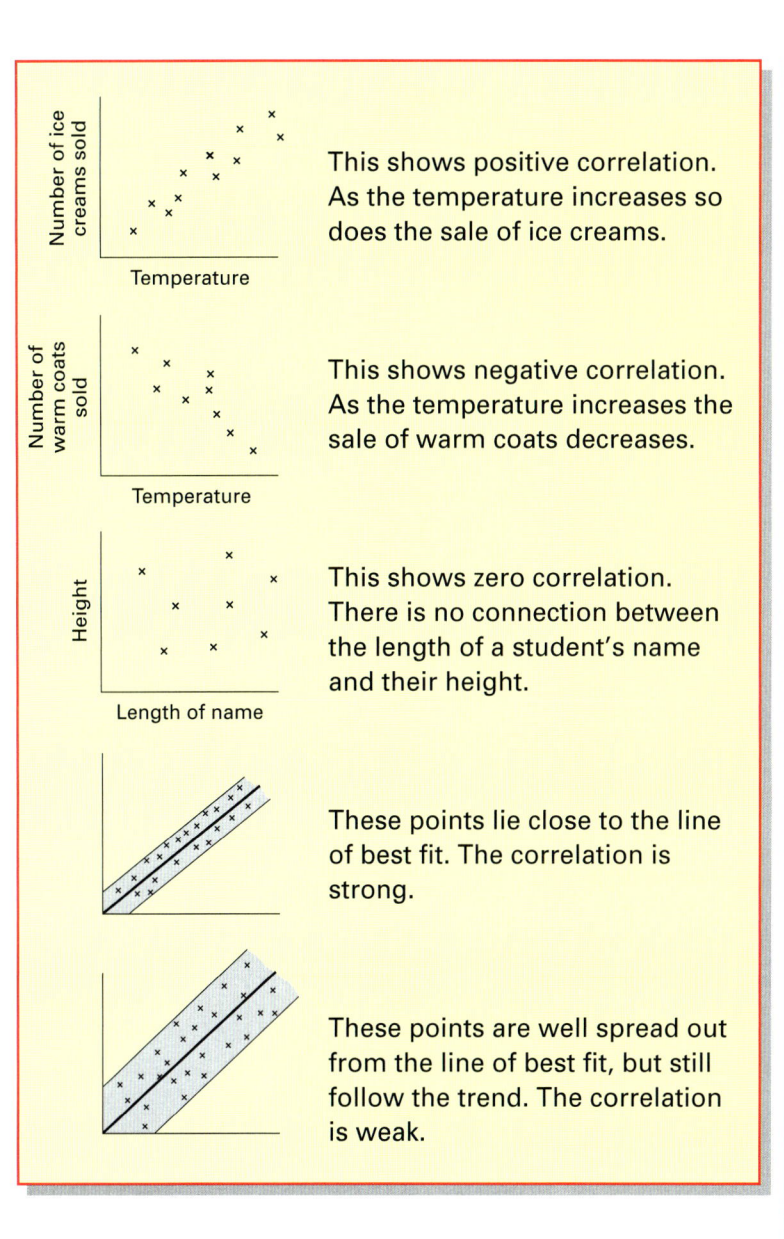

This shows positive correlation. As the temperature increases so does the sale of ice creams.

This shows negative correlation. As the temperature increases the sale of warm coats decreases.

This shows zero correlation. There is no connection between the length of a student's name and their height.

These points lie close to the line of best fit. The correlation is strong.

These points are well spread out from the line of best fit, but still follow the trend. The correlation is weak.

Notes

Chapter 3 pages 54–58

☐ Histograms

A **histogram** looks like a bar chart, but there are some important differences.
- It can only be used for **continuous** numerical data.
- Data shown on a histogram is always grouped.
- The scale along the bottom must be labelled like a graph scale.

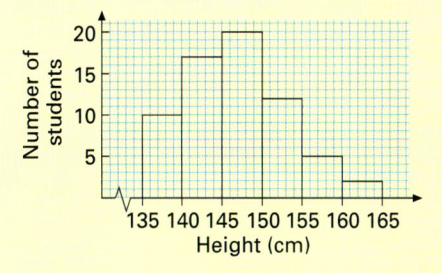

This histogram shows the heights of a group of students.

Continuous data can take any value in a given range.
Discrete data can only take certain values. You can't draw a histogram to show favourite football teams.

Make the widths of the groups the same. The height of the bar tells you the number in each group.

17 students are between 140 and 145 cm tall.

19 students are taller than 150 cm.

There are 66 students altogether in this group.

Chapter 3 pages 58–61

Frequency polygons

Frequency polygons are often used to compare two sets of data.

You use straight lines to join up the mid points of the tops of the bars of a histogram. This makes a frequency polygon.

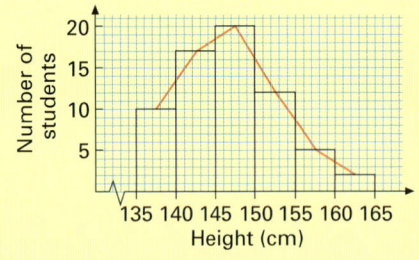

This diagram shows the above histogram with the frequency polygon drawn in red.

The frequency polygon shows the **trend**. The trend shows how the data is changing.

You can draw a frequency polygon without first drawing the histogram.

Example
Draw a frequency polygon to show the heights of students given by this table.

Height	135<x≤140	140<x≤145	145<x≤150	150<x≤155	155<x≤160
Number of students	10	18	22	12	8
Mid point	137.5	142.5	147.5	152.5	157.5

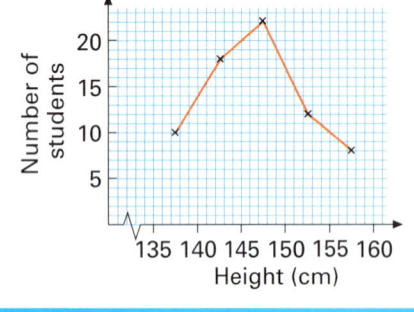

Notes

You must use straight lines to join the mid points of the tops of the bars.

Work out the mid point of each group.

Plot the mid points and join them with a straight line.

Remember to label the axes. The vertical axis shows the number of students. The horizontal axis shows the heights of the students.

Chapter 3 pages 61–66

TEST YOURSELF

1 The table gives the weights and heights of 15 boys.
   a Draw a scatter graph for the data.
   b Draw the line of best fit.
   c Estimate the weight of a boy who is 160 cm tall.

Height (cm)	158	159	157	165	161	162	159	160	164	156	159	162	170	147	155
Weight (kg)	60	61	63	66	59	62	58	60	62	60	57	61	65	56	58

2 The table gives the results of 10 pupils in geography and history tests.
   Draw a scatter graph for these results. Is there any correlation between these results?

Geography (%)	68	90	42	50	86	84	78	80	50	65
History (%)	60	85	40	41	75	89	65	78	46	80

Averages

☐ Mean, mode and median

An **average** is a value that you use to represent a set of data. It is a single value that tells you about the size of the data. There are three types of average:

- The **mean** is often regarded as the best average. You use every value to calculate the mean but it can be distorted by extreme values.
  To find the mean of a set of data:
  (1) Find the total of all the data values.
  (2) Divide the total by the number of data values.

- The **mode** is the easiest to find.
  The mode is the most common or most popular data value. It is sometimes called the **modal value**.

- The **median** is a good measure to use if you have extreme values that could distort your average.
  To find the median you put all the data values in order of size. The median is then the value in the middle.

This table shows the number of children per family in a class of thirty children.

Number of children	Number of families
1	5
2	12
3	10
4	3
	Total = 30

The **modal** number of children per family is the number with the highest frequency. The mode is 2.

The **median** is the middle value. There are 30 data items. So $(30 + 1) \div 2 = 15\frac{1}{2}$. The median is the $15\frac{1}{2}$th value. You want the value that is halfway between the 15th and the 16th terms.

Number of children	Number of families	Running total
1	5	5
2	12	5 + 12 = 17
3	10	
4	3	
	Total = 30	

The 15th and 16th terms must both be 2. So the median is 2.

Notes

It is important that you chose the most appropriate average for the question you are answering.

Chapter 16 pages 338–348

There are more families with two children than any other number.

The median of n values is the $(n + 1) \div 2$ th value.

You could write out all 30 values in order to find the 15th and 16th values. A quicker method is to write down a running total.

By the time you have listed all the 2s you will have 17 terms. So the 15th and 16th terms must both be 2.

The **mean** is $\frac{\text{Total number of children}}{\text{Total number of families}}$.

You need to find the total number of children. Add another column to your table like this:

Number of children	Number of families (Frequency)	Children × Frequency
1	5	1 × 5 = 5
2	12	2 × 12 = 24
3	10	3 × 10 = 30
4	3	4 × 3 = 12
	Total = 30	Total = 71

The mean number of children per family is $\frac{71}{30}$ = 2.3666...

= 2.4 to 1 dp

☐ Estimating the mean, modal group and range for grouped data

When you are dealing with a lot of data you can put the data into groups. This makes the data easier to deal with but you can only estimate averages.

Mark recorded the number of words in each sentence in a passage in the book he was reading.

Words	Frequency
1–5	8
6–10	15
11–15	14
16–20	10
21–25	7
26–30	5
31–35	1
Total	60

Words	Mid point (x)	Frequency (f)	f × x
1–5	3	8	24
6–10	8	15	120
11–15	13	14	182
16–20	18	10	180
21–25	23	7	161
26–30	28	5	140
31–35	33	1	33
Total		60	840

Notes

Even though it is impossible to have 2.4 children, the mean gives a value that represents the data. It is more than 2 and allows for the high number of families with three children.

The groupings can be given in different ways.
10 < x ≤ 20 means 10 is not included in the group, but 20 is included. 15 is the middle value.
10 ≤ x < 20 means 10 is included in the group, but 20 is not included. The middle value is 15.
10–, 20–, 30–, means that the first group includes values from 10 up to, but not including 20. The middle value is still 15.
–10, –20, –30, means that the first group is values up to and including 10. The second group is values up to and including 20, but 10 is not included. The middle value of this second group is 15.

Eight sentences contained between one and five words. You do not know exactly how many words were in each sentence. To work out an estimate for the mean you have to assume that all eight sentences contained the number of words in the middle of the group. This middle value is = $\frac{1+5}{2}$ = 3

Add two extra columns to your table. Complete the column showing the mid values. You have assumed that eight sentences each contained three words.
This gives a total of 8 × 3 = 24 words. Similarly, you have assumed that 15 sentences each contained eight words. This gives 15 × 8 = 120 words.

You can only estimate the mean as you do not know exactly how many words there were in each sentence.

Mean = $\frac{\text{Total number of words}}{\text{Total number of sentences}} = \frac{840}{60} = 14$

So 14 is the estimate for the mean.

When data is grouped you cannot tell which value is the most common. You can only say which group contains the most values. This is called the **modal group**.

For the data given in the table the modal group is 6 to 10 words.

You can estimate the range for this data by subtracting the smallest possible value from the largest possible value.

The largest possible value is 35 words per sentence and the smallest is one word per sentence.

So an estimate for the range is 34 words.

Notes

This mean has been calculated by assuming that all the sentences contain the middle number of words.

If a question asks for the estimate of the mean it is telling you to use this method and not just guess a rough answer.

The group 6–10 has the highest frequency. It is therefore the modal group.

The range is the difference between the largest value and the smallest value.

Chapter 16 pages 349–353

TEST YOURSELF

1 Work out the mean, median and mode for the following sets of numbers.
  a 2, 5, 6, 7, 7, 9
  b 16, 20, 14, 25, 17, 26, 16, 21, 16, 19

2 The table shows the number of letters delivered to the houses in Acacia Avenue.

Number of letters	Frequency
0	5
1	8
2	12
3	16
4	22
5	13
6	4
Total	80

Find:
a the mean
b the modal number
c the median number of letters delivered to each house

3 This table shows the number of minutes a train was late on 30 occasions.

Minutes late	Frequency
$0 \leqslant t < 2$	12
$2 \leqslant t < 4$	8
$4 \leqslant t < 6$	5
$6 \leqslant t < 8$	2
$8 \leqslant t < 10$	3
Total	30

a Find the mean number of minutes the train is late.
b What is the modal group?

Comparing data

☐ Comparing data using average and spread

The **mean** and the **median** tell you how big the values are in a data set on average.

The **range** tells you how spread out the data values are.

To compare two sets of data you need to use both an average value and a measure of spread.

The number of goals scored by James and Andrew in their last five football games were:

James   3   2   0   0   4
Andrew   2   1   2   1   1

James' mean score is 1.8 goals and Andrew's mean score is 1.4 goals.

The range of James' scores is 4 and the range of Andrew's scores is 1.

Although James has a slightly higher mean score he is less consistent than Andrew as he has a greater range. This means he may score a lot of goals but also he may score very few. Andrew will score consistently.

☐ Interquartile range

The range is a simple measure of spread, considering only the highest and lowest values. It can be badly affected by a single extreme value.

The **interquartile range** measures the spread of the middle half of the data. So it is not affected by extreme values.

The **lower quartile** is the value one-quarter of the way through the data.

The **upper quartile** is the value three-quarters of the way through the data.

The interquartile range = upper quartile – lower quartile.

To find the interquartile range:
(1) You must write the data in order.
(2) Find the position of the median.
(3) Look at the data to the left of this position.
    The lower quartile is the median of this half of the data.
(4) Look at the data to the right of the median.
    The upper quartile is the median of this half of the data.

4   **5**   6   8   9   **12**   13

lower quartile = 5   median = 8   upper quartile = 12   interquartile range = 12 – 5 = 7

3   4   4   6   9   9   12   13

lower quartile = 4   median = $\frac{6+9}{2}$ = 7.5   upper quartile = $\frac{9+12}{2}$ = 10.5   interquartile range = 10.5 – 4 = 6.5

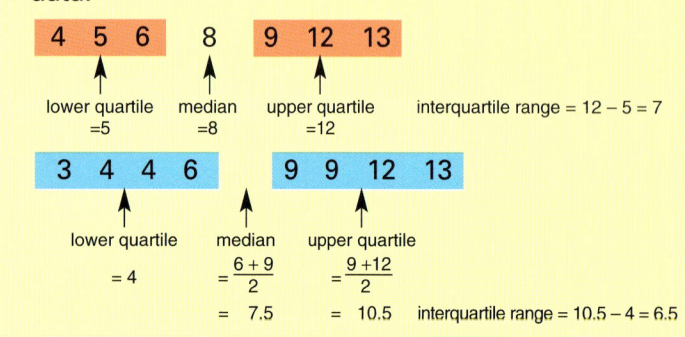

Notes

Generally the mean and the range are used to make a simple comparison between two sets of data.

James:

Mean = $\frac{3+2+0+0+4}{5} = 1.8$

Range = 4 – 0 = 4

Andrew:

Mean = $\frac{2+1+2+1+1}{5} = 1.4$

Range = 2 – 1 = 1

You know that the median is the value half way through the data, and it is not affected by extreme values.

Chapter 25 pages 125–126

If there are two numbers in the middle of the data you must add them together and divide by 2 to find the median.

The same method is used to calculate the quartiles.

The interquartile range includes the middle half of all the data values.

☐ Cumulative frequency

Cumulative frequency is a running total.

This table shows the ages of the residents of a street.

Ages (Years)	Frequency	Cumulative Frequency
< 5	10	10
< 15	10	20 (10 + 10)
< 20	14	34 (20 + 14)
< 25	29	63 (34 + 29)
< 35	34	97 (63 + 34)
< 45	36	133 (97 + 36)
< 60	23	156 (133 + 23)
< 70	12	168 (156 + 12)
< 90	2	170 (168 + 2)

This information can be shown on a graph, called a **cumulative frequency diagram**.

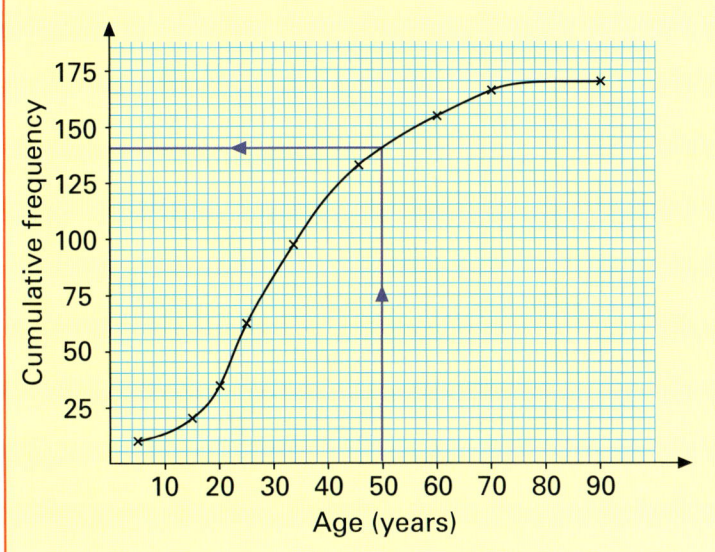

Notes

This diagram shows how the cumulative frequency changes as the data values increase. The data is shown on a continuous scale on the horizontal axis. The cumulative frequency is shown on the vertical scale.

To estimate the number of people who are over 50 years of age find 50 on the horizontal axis. Go up to the curve and across and read off the value on the cumulative frequency axis.
This tells you that there are 140 people who are aged under 50 years.
To find the number who are over 50 you must subtract 140 from the total number of people (170).
170 − 140 = 30.
So there are 30 people over 50 years old.

You must show the lines going up and across.

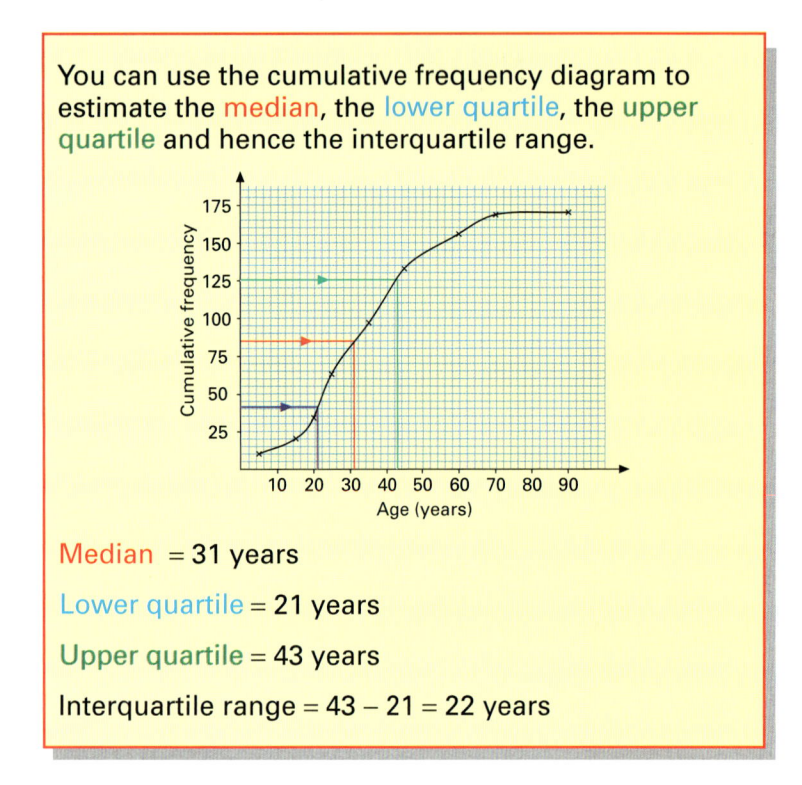

You can use the cumulative frequency diagram to estimate the median, the lower quartile, the upper quartile and hence the interquartile range.

Median = 31 years

Lower quartile = 21 years

Upper quartile = 43 years

Interquartile range = 43 − 21 = 22 years

☐ **Using the median and interquartile range to compare data**

You can compare two sets of data by comparing the average and a measure of spread. You have already seen the mean and range used to do this. By using the interquartile range as the measure of spread a more accurate comparison can be made.
A small interquartile range tells you that the middle half of the data are closely grouped together. Extreme values do not distort this measure of spread.

Notes

To estimate the median:
(1) Divide the total cumulative frequency by 2.
(2) Find this point on the cumulative frequency axis.
(3) Draw a line across to the curve and down to the horizontal axis.
(4) Read off the estimate of the median.

To estimate the lower quartile:
(1) Divide the total cumulative frequency by 4.
(2) Find this point on the cumulative frequency axis. (Here it is 42.5)
(3) Draw lines as you did for the median.
(4) Read off the value of the lower quartile.

To estimate the upper quartile:
(1) Divide the total cumulative frequency by 4 and multiply by 3.
(2) Find this point on the cumulative frequency axis. (Here it is 127.5)
(3) Draw lines as you did for the median.
(4) Read off the value of the upper quartile.

Chapter 25 pages 127–139

TEST YOURSELF

1 The number of wickets taken by John and Martin in their last six cricket matches is shown in the table.

John   3   4   3   2   4   3
Martin 5   1   1   2   5   0

Compare their results.
Who would you pick for your team?

2 Find the median and the interquartile range of each of the following sets of data.

a 5, 10, 12, 13, 14, 18, 21
b 8, 8, 9, 15, 16, 32

3 These are the marks scored by a group of 100 students in a test.

Marks	Frequency
1–10	6
11–20	14
21–30	18
31–40	42
41–50	20

Draw a cumulative frequency diagram.
Use your diagram to find an estimate for the median and the interquartile range.

Simple probability

☐ Probability scales

Probability tells you how likely something is to happen.

Words such as impossible, unlikely and very likely are often used to describe probability. A numerical scale is used to measure probability more accurately.

An event that is impossible has a probability of 0.

An event that is certain to happen has a probability of 1.

All probabilities are measured on a scale ranging from 0 to 1.

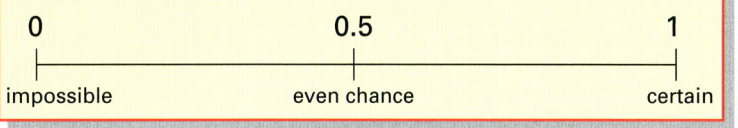

```
0                    0.5                    1
|--------------------|--------------------|
impossible       even chance          certain
```

☐ Fairness and bias – equally likely

In probability something is **fair** if it is no more, or less, likely to happen than another event.
If a coin is described as fair you are **equally likely** to get a head or a tail when the coin is thrown.

This spinner is not fair as you are more likely to get red than blue.

☐ Probabilities add up to one

Probabilities always add up to one.
There are 5 blue counters and 3 green counters in a bag. One counter is chosen at random and taken out of the bag.

There are 8 counters altogether so you can draw a scale using eighths. The probability that a blue counter is picked is $\frac{5}{8}$.

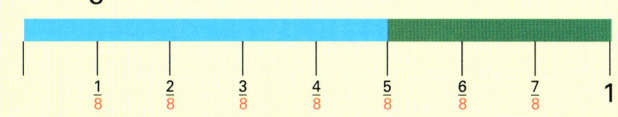

$$\frac{1}{8} \quad \frac{2}{8} \quad \frac{3}{8} \quad \frac{4}{8} \quad \frac{5}{8} \quad \frac{6}{8} \quad \frac{7}{8} \quad 1$$

The probability of choosing a green counter is $\frac{3}{8}$.

This is written $P(\text{green}) = \frac{3}{8}$.

This is also the probability of not getting a blue.
So $P(\text{not blue}) = \frac{3}{8}$.

These probabilities add to 1 so you can write
$P(\text{not blue}) = 1 - P(\text{blue})$
$= 1 - \frac{5}{8} = \frac{3}{8}$

Notes

The probability that the sun will rise tomorrow is certain. It has probability of 1.

There is an even chance you will get a head when you throw a fair coin. The probability of this is 0.5 or $\frac{1}{2}$.

You have the same chance to get a head or a tail.

Five sections are shaded red, but only three sections are shaded blue.
Red and blue are not equally likely with this spinner.

You can write probabilities as fractions, decimals or percentages.

You can colour the first five eighths of the scale blue. The rest of the scale must be green.

Three eighths have been shaded green.

Chapter 10 pages 216–222 →

☐ Finding probabilities

The **probability of an event A**

= $\dfrac{\text{the number of ways that the event A can happen}}{\text{the total number of events}}$

If you roll this spinner there are four possible colours you could get.

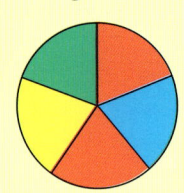

There are five equal sections, two of which are red.

$P(B) = \dfrac{1}{5}$ as only one of the five sections is blue.

$P(R) = \dfrac{2}{5}$ as two of the five sections are red.

The probability of not getting blue = $\dfrac{4}{5}$ as there are four sections which are not shaded blue.

So B' means that you get red, yellow or green. B' is the event 'not B'.

$P(B') = 1 - P(B)$

So the probability of not getting a blue is

$P(B') = 1 - \dfrac{1}{5} = \dfrac{4}{5}$

Notes

An event is one thing that can happen in a probability experiment. It is one of the possible outcomes.

B is the event 'spinner landing on blue'

R is the event 'spinner landing on red'

Chapter 10 pages 222–227

☐ Relative frequency

The **frequency** of an event is the number of times it happens.

The **relative frequency** of an event

= $\dfrac{\text{frequency of the event}}{\text{total frequency}}$

The relative frequency gives an estimate of the probability.

John throws a coin sixty times. The table shows his results.

	Frequency
Head	40
Tail	20

The relative frequency of a head = $\dfrac{40}{60} = \dfrac{2}{3}$

The relative frequency of a tail = $\dfrac{20}{60} = \dfrac{1}{3}$

Relative frequency is used to estimate probability when you have the results of an experiment.

If you repeat the experiment a large number of times you find a more accurate estimate for the probability. The relative frequency becomes a better estimate of probability as you do the experiment more times.

Chapter 10 pages 228–229

Sample space diagrams

A **sample space diagram** is a table showing all the possible outcomes of a probability experiment.

Jenny throws a coin and spins a four-sided dice. The table shows all the possible outcomes.

		Dice			
		1	2	3	4
Coin	Head	H, 1	H, 2	H, 3	H, 4
	Tail	T, 1	T, 2	T, 3	T, 4

There are eight possible outcomes. They are all equally likely.

The probability of getting a Tail and a 3 is $\frac{1}{8}$

Notes

Each thing that can happen is called an outcome.

A sample space diagram makes it easy to see all the outcomes.

Chapter 21 pages 44–46

Expected number

You can work out how many times an event is likely to happen when you repeat an experiment.

The **expected number** = number of trials × probability

John and Andrew play chess. The probability that John wins a game of chess against Andrew is 0.65 They play each other 20 times.

So you would expect John to win 20 × 0.65 = 13 games.

Work out the probability that the event happens once. Then multiply by the number of times the experiment is repeated.

Methods of finding probability

There are three methods of finding probability.

Method 1: Use equally likely outcomes

Method 2: Carry out an experiment

Method 3: Look at previous data

E.g. to find the probability of getting a four on a fair dice.
E.g. to find the probability that a drawing pin will land point up.
E.g. to find the probability that there will be more than 10 cm rain in August.

TEST YOURSELF

1. Jim and Janet are playing a game. They throw a dice to see who goes first. Jim will go first if he throws a prime number. Janet will go first if the number she throws is not prime. Is this fair? Explain your answer.

2. A fair six-sided dice is thrown. What is the probability that the number scored will:
   a be a 5
   b be more than 4
   c be less than 8.

3. A biased dice is thrown 100 times. This table shows the results.

Score	1	2	3	4	5	6
Frequency	12	14	25	20	14	15

   a Work out the relative frequency of each score.
   b If the dice is thrown 600 times how many times would you expect to get a 3?

93

Laws of probability

☐ Independent events

Two events are **independent** if the outcome of one has no effect on the outcome of the other.

If two events A and B are independent then the probability of them both happening is called P(A and B).

P(A and B) = P(A) × P(B)

You throw a dice and spin a coin. If you show the outcomes on a probability space diagram you can see that

$P(\text{Head and } 5) = \frac{1}{12}$.

Using independent events: $P(\text{Head and } 5) = \frac{1}{2} \times \frac{1}{6} = \frac{1}{12}$

☐ Probability of an event happening more than once

You can use independent events to find the probability of an event happening more than once.

You throw a coin three times. You want to work out the probability of getting three tails.

The probability of getting a tail on the first throw is $\frac{1}{2}$.

Each throw is independent.

$P(\text{three tails}) = \frac{1}{2} \times \frac{1}{2} \times \frac{1}{2} = \frac{1}{8}$

☐ Mutually exclusive events

Events are **mutually exclusive** if they cannot happen at the same time.

For two mutually exclusive events A and B, the probability that *either* A *or* B will occur, can be found by adding together their probabilities.

P(A or B) = P(A) + P(B)

A ten-sided dice, numbered 1 to 10, is thrown. F is the event 'getting a 5', and E is the event 'getting an even number'. The events F and E are mutually exclusive.

$P(F) = \frac{1}{10}$ and $P(E) = \frac{1}{2}$

So, $P(F \text{ or } E) = \frac{1}{10} + \frac{1}{2} = \frac{6}{10} = \frac{3}{5}$

Notes

If you roll a fair dice you can get a 1, 2, 3, 4, 5 or 6. If you throw a coin you can get a head or a tail. The number you get on the dice has no effect on whether you get a head or tail on the coin.
Throwing a coin and rolling a dice are independent events.

	1	2	3	4	5	6
Head	H,1	H,2	H,3	H,4	H,5	H,6
Tail	T,1	T,2	T,3	T,4	T,5	T,6

This is the same answer as you get using the sample space diagram.
This method is much quicker.

Multiply probabilities when questions ask for something *and* something else, or *both* things happening.

'AND = ×'

P(3 tails) = P(tail and tail and tail)
         = P(tail) × P(tail) × P(tail)

Chapter 21 pages 49–55

When you throw a coin it can land with a head showing or with a tail showing. It cannot land showing both a head and a tail at the same time.
The events heads and tails are mutually exclusive.

If an even number is thrown, then you cannot have a five showing. These events are mutually exclusive, as five is not an even number.

TEST YOURSELF

1 The events A and B are independent. P(A) = 0.4 and P(B) = 0.2. Find P(A and B).

2 A coin is thrown and a fair dice is rolled. Find:
   a the probability that the coin lands heads and the dice shows a four.
   b the probability that you get a tail and an even number.

Tree diagrams

☐ Finding probabilities using tree diagrams

> You can use **tree diagrams** to show the outcomes of two or more events. Each branch represents a possible outcome for one event. The probability for each event is written along the branch. The final outcome depends on the route followed along the branches.

Notes

Always use a pencil and a ruler to draw tree diagrams. This will help you to make them neater and easier to read.

Chapter 31 pages 264–269

Examples

The probability that a student chosen at random is left-handed is 0.1. Two students are chosen at random.

a Show all the possible outcomes on a tree diagram.
b Find the probability that both students are left-handed.
c Find the probability that only one of the students is left-handed.

a
1st student	2nd student		Probability
0.1 left	0.1 left	left, left	0.1 × 0.1 = 0.01
	0.9 right	left, right	0.1 × 0.9 = 0.09
0.9 right	0.1 left	right, left	0.9 × 0.1 = 0.09
	0.9 right	right, right	0.9 × 0.9 = 0.81

The first set of branches shows that the 1st student can either be right-handed or left-handed.
The second set of branches shows that the 2nd student can also be either right-hand or left-handed.

Each route through the tree gives a different outcome. These outcomes are shown to the right of the diagram.

b The red path shows the outcome 'both students are left-handed'.

You can work out the probability of this outcome by multiplying together the probabilities on the branches.

P(both students are left-handed) = 0.1 × 0.1 = 0.01

The top blue path gives the first student being left-handed and the second student is right-handed. The lower blue path gives the outcome of only the second student being left-handed.

c Each of the blue paths leads to an outcome where one of the students is left-handed. You must add together the probabilities of both of these outcomes to give the probability that only one student is left-handed.

P(one student is left-handed) = 0.09 + 0.09 = 0.18

Remember:
You multiply the probabilities along the branches.
You add the probabilities when more than one path is used.

TEST YOURSELF

1 Jim catches a bus to the station and then catches a train to work. The probability that Jim's bus is late is 0.2. The probability that the train is late is 0.25.
Use a tree diagram to find:
a the probability that both the train and the bus are not late
b the probability that the train is late but the bus is on time.

2 Ann and Juliet are learning archery. The probability that Ann hits the target is $\frac{3}{4}$ and the probability that Juliet hits the target is $\frac{4}{5}$.
a Draw a tree diagram to show all the possible outcomes.
b Find the probability that both girls hit the target.
c Find the probability that only one girl hits the target.

☐ Drawing appropriate tree diagrams

> Sometimes a tree diagram can take a long time to draw if all the outcomes are included. You can simplify them by drawing only the paths you actually need.

Notes

Example

When playing a board game you must throw two dice. Find the probability of getting two fours.

For each dice here are six possible outcomes: 1, 2, 3, 4, 5 and 6.

The outcome 'not a 4' includes the outcomes 1, 2, 3, 5 and 6.

You are only interested in the outcomes which give a four, so you only need to draw branches showing 'a 4' or 'not a 4'.

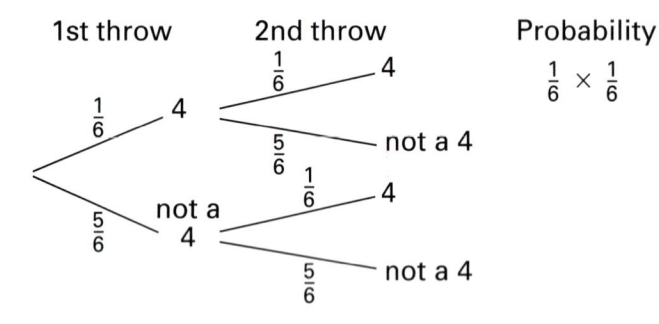

1st throw   2nd throw   Probability

- $\frac{1}{6}$ → 4
  - $\frac{1}{6}$ → 4 $\frac{1}{6} \times \frac{1}{6}$
  - $\frac{5}{6}$ → not a 4
- $\frac{5}{6}$ → not a 4
  - $\frac{1}{6}$ → 4
  - $\frac{5}{6}$ → not a 4

P two fours $= \frac{1}{6} \times \frac{1}{6} = \frac{1}{36}$

> Sometimes one of the paths of a tree diagram stops before the others.

If Steve makes a sale at the first shop he visits he will not call at the second or third shop.

Example

Steve is selling soap powder. The probability that he makes a sale is 0.7. He has up to three shops to visit, but will stop when he makes his first sale.
a Draw a tree diagram to show the possible outcomes.
b Find the probability that Steve makes his first sale at the second shop.

a   1st Shop   2nd Shop

- 0.7 → Sale
- 0.3 → No sale
  - 0.7 → Sale
  - 0.3 → No sale
    - 0.7 → Sale
    - 0.3 → No sale

The top path stops because Steve has made a sale and therefore does not need to visit the next shop.

b P(first sale at second shop)
$= P(\text{No sale}) \times P(\text{Sale})$
$= 0.3 \times 0.7$
$= 0.21$

Chapter 31 pages 270–271

☐ Changing probabilities

> You must take care when completing the probabilities on a tree diagram. They are not always the same on each path.

Example

Petra can either cycle or walk to school. The probability that she cycles is 0.7. If she cycles to school the probability that she is late is 0.2. If she walks to school the probability that she is late is 0.4. By drawing a tree diagram find the probability that Petra is late for school.

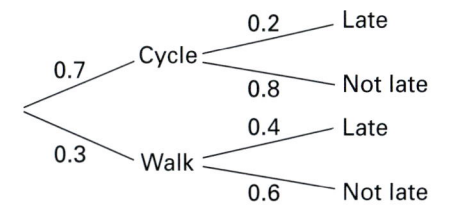

```
         0.2 — Late
    Cycle
0.7      0.8 — Not late
         0.4 — Late
0.3  Walk
         0.6 — Not late
```

P(Petra is late for school) = (0.7 × 0.2) + (0.3 × 0.4)
= 0.14 × 0.12
= 0.26

☐ Questions using the words 'at least one'

> When solving probability questions you should always look out for the phrase **'at least one'**. For example, when three coins are thrown, what is the probability of getting at least one head?
>
> The events 'at least one head' and 'no heads' are mutually exclusive. These events also include all the possible outcomes – nothing else is possible.
>
> Either there are no heads or there is at least one head.
> So P(at least one head) = 1 − P(no heads)
>
> $= 1 - \frac{1}{2} \times \frac{1}{2} \times \frac{1}{2}$
>
> $= 1 - \frac{1}{8}$
>
> $= \frac{7}{8}$

Notes

The probability that Petra is late is different for walking and cycling.
The top half of the tree diagram shows the outcomes when Petra cycles to school. In this case the probability that she is late is 0.2
The lower half shows the outcomes when Petra walks to school. Here the probability that she is late is 0.4

The probability that Petra is late is found by adding together the probability that she cycles and is late, and the probability that she walks and is late.

> Chapter 31 pages 272–275

Mutually exclusive events cannot both happen at the same time.

When one coin is thrown the probability of not getting a head is $\frac{1}{2}$.

The probability of getting no heads when three coins are thrown is $\frac{1}{2} \times \frac{1}{2} \times \frac{1}{2}$.

This is the same as the probability of getting three tails.
i.e. P(no heads) = P(3 tails)

> Chapter 31 pages 276–282

TEST YOURSELF

1. Sanjay spins this spinner twice.
   Draw a tree diagram and find the probability that he gets:
   a red on each spin
   b red on only one spin

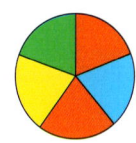

2. Simon catches the bus to college. The probability he catches the early bus is 0.6, otherwise he catches the later bus. If he catches the early bus then the probability that he is late for college is 0.15. The probability that he is late for college if he catches the later bus is 0.6. Use a tree diagram to find the probability that Simon:
   a catches the early bus and arrives at college on time
   b arrives at college on time.

Practice questions

1 The number of goals scored by Mulchester Rovers in each of the first ten matches of the season was

$$3, \ 1, \ 1, \ 2, \ 0, \ 1, \ 2, \ 3, \ 4, \ 1$$

What was the:

a modal number of goals scored (1)

b median number of goals scored (3)

c mean number of goals scored? (3)

NICCEA, 1999, Paper G60-3I

2 A number of women do aerobics for one minute.
Their ages and pulse rates are shown in the table.

Age (years)	16	17	22	25	38	42	43	50
Pulse rate (per minute)	82	78	83	90	99	97	108	107

a Copy the axes below. Use this information to draw a scatter graph. (2)

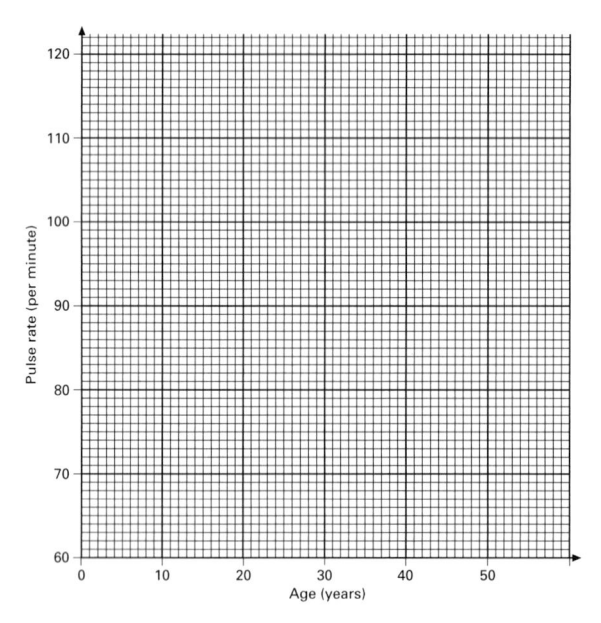

b What type of correlation is there between the ages and pulse rates of these women? (1)

c Draw a line of best fit. (1)

d Betty is 35 years old. Estimate her pulse rate after doing aerobics for one minute. (1)

SEG, 1999, Paper 2500/13

3 A box contains buttons.
The buttons have two, three or four holes, as shown.
The buttons are coloured white or red or green.

A button is taken at random from the box.
The table shows the probabilities of the numbers of holes and the colours of the buttons.

		Number of holes		
		2	3	4
Colour	White	0.3	0.2	0
	Red	0.1	0	0.2
	Green	0	0.1	0.1

a A button is taken from the box at random.

  i What is the probability that it is red with two holes? (1)

  ii What is the probability that it has two holes? (1)

  iii What is the probability that it is red or has two holes (or both?) (1)

b The box contains 50 buttons.

  How many buttons have four holes? (2)

SEG, 1999, Paper 2500/13

4 On his way to work, Nick goes through a set of traffic lights and then passes over a level crossing.
Over a period of time, Nick has estimated the probability of stopping at each of these.
The probability that he has to stop at the traffic lights is $\frac{2}{3}$.
The probability that he has to stop at the level crossing is $\frac{1}{5}$.
These probabilities are independent.

  a Construct a tree diagram to show this information. (3)

  b Calculate the probability that Nick will not have to stop at either the lights or the level crossing on his way to work. (2)

OCR, 1999, Paper 1664/4

ANSWERS

Number

Number skills, page 3

1 a Nine million and seventy thousand five hundred and one.
  b Seventy million four hundred thousand and seventy six

2 a 287.036 kg   **b** 2.672 m
  c 4.404   **d** 49.5

3 a 2198.3   **b** 56.46 (2 dp)

4 a 4   **b** 22   **c** 8   **d** 290
  e 4   **f** 113 **g** 928 **h** 21.2 (3 sf)

page 5

1 (1) a 1260   **b** 4460
     c 5450   **d** 9900

  (2) a 1000   **b** 4000
     c 5000   **d** 10 000

2 a 68.42 g   **b** 4.37 t   **c** 0.09 kg

3 a 0.0699   **b** 55 000

4 a Estimate 32
      Actual   31.92
  b Estimate 7
      Actual   7.26 (3sf)
  c Estimate 17
      Actual   16.8
  d Estimate 6
      Actual   6.28
  e Estimate 35 000
      Actual   32 352
  f Estimate 40
      Actual   44.7 (3sf)

5 a UB = 12.655   **b** UB = 17.379025
     LB = 12.645   LB = 17.379015

6 a 0.8   **b** 11.1%

Types of number, page 7

1 a 36, 45, 54, 63
  b 15, 30, 45, 60
  c 40
  d 36
  e 1, 2, 3, 4, 6, 9, 12, 18, 36
  f $2 \times 2 \times 2 \times 3 \times 3 = 2^3 \times 3^2$
  g $2 \times 3^2 \times 5 \times 7$
  h 21, 28, 36, 45
  i 49, 64, 81, 100, 121

2 a prime numbers
  b multiples of three
  c triangle numbers
  d square numbers
  e factors of 18
  f multiples of 2 or even numbers
  g square root
  h odd numbers
  i square
  j factors of 32

Negative numbers, page 9

1 −162°C, −11°C, −6°C, 53°C

2 a −23   **b** 2   **c** −15
  d 3   **e** −16   **f** −5
  g −38 **h** −47   **i** −665

3 a −18   **b** 84   **c** 36
  d −8   **e** −343 **f** $-\frac{1}{2}$

4 a −5.4 **b** 5   **c** 0.328 3 sf

Ratio, page 11

1 5:1

2 155 kg oats
   62 kg wheat
   31 kg maize

3 180g pack for £1.98

4 224g for 19p

5 a 64p   **b** 128p   **c** 28

Fractions, decimals and percentages, page 12

1 a $\frac{3}{2}$ **b** $\frac{8}{3}$ **c** $\frac{15}{4}$
  d $\frac{17}{5}$ **e** $\frac{29}{6}$ **f** $\frac{79}{16}$

2 a $2\frac{1}{2}$ **b** $4\frac{2}{3}$ **c** $3\frac{3}{4}$
  d $4\frac{1}{5}$ **e** $2\frac{5}{8}$ **f** $3\frac{1}{12}$
  g $3\frac{1}{7}$ **h** $3\frac{8}{9}$ **i** $1\frac{20}{25} = 1\frac{4}{5}$

3 a $\frac{1}{2} = \frac{4}{8}$ **b** $\frac{3}{8} = \frac{6}{16}$ **c** $\frac{4}{5} = \frac{8}{10}$
  d $\frac{3}{7} = \frac{6}{14}$ **e** $\frac{14}{25} = \frac{56}{100}$ **f** $\frac{8}{9} = \frac{320}{360}$

4 a $\frac{1}{2}$ **b** $\frac{3}{4}$ **c** $\frac{5}{8}$
  d $\frac{1}{4}$ **e** $\frac{1}{4}$ **f** $\frac{2}{3}$
  g $\frac{1}{4}$ **h** $\frac{2}{5}$ **i** $\frac{1}{3}$

page 13

1 a 14   **b** 24   **c** 18
  d 10   **e** 30   **f** 304
  g 60   **h** 672 **i** 128

100

2
a $\frac{1}{16}$ b $\frac{1}{2}$ c $1\frac{1}{2}$
d $\frac{5}{8}$ e $1\frac{2}{3}$ f $\frac{3}{5}$
g $\frac{2}{17}$ h $\frac{3}{4}$ i $\frac{1}{3}$

3
a $1\frac{1}{4}$ b $\frac{7}{16}$ c $1\frac{1}{16}$
d $\frac{3}{10}$ e $1\frac{1}{2}$ f $\frac{13}{20}$
g $\frac{1}{6}$ h $3\frac{1}{8}$ i $\frac{17}{63}$

4
a $3\frac{3}{4}$ b $2\frac{3}{16}$ c $9\frac{1}{6}$
d $3\frac{1}{2}$ e $9\frac{11}{20}$ f $1\frac{10}{21}$

page 14

1 $\frac{5}{7}$

2
a $\frac{2}{5}$ b $\frac{3}{20}$ c $\frac{3}{5}$
d 2   e $1\frac{1}{6}$ f $1\frac{1}{3}$

3
a $1\frac{1}{5}$ b $8\frac{4}{5}$ c $13\frac{3}{4}$
d 1   e $8\frac{3}{4}$ f $23\frac{1}{3}$
g 10   h $\frac{11}{16}$ i 2
j $1\frac{1}{2}$ k $2\frac{2}{3}$ l $11\frac{1}{9}$

page 16

1 a 0.6   b 0.25   c $0.\dot{6}$ d 0.375

2 a 50%   b 5%   c 8%   d 58%

3 a 40%   b 75%   c 87.5%   d 71.4% (3 sf)

4 a 0.25   b 0.7   c 0.07   d 0.77

5
a $\frac{3}{10}$ b $\frac{7}{10}$ c $\frac{1}{100}$ d $\frac{2}{25}$
e $\frac{47}{100}$ f $\frac{3}{4}$ g $\frac{33}{50}$ or $\frac{2}{3}$ h $\frac{2}{250}$

6 a $\frac{1}{4}$ b $\frac{2}{5}$ c $\frac{13}{20}$ d $\frac{6}{25}$

7 0.4 and $\frac{2}{5}$ and 40%
0.21 and 21%
$\frac{1}{25}$ and 0.04 and 4%
$\frac{21}{50}$ and 42% and 0.42
0.84 and $\frac{21}{25}$

Using percentages, page 17

1 a 1.42   b 0.64

2 a £92   b £32.40

3 a £1170   b £5059.20
c £1376   d £7065.60

page 18

1 a £17.50   b £10.50   c £43.75

2 a £37.60
b £5287.50
c £1133.88 (nearest penny)

3 a £14000   b £249.50

page 20

1 a 7.65%   b 8.3%

2 a £1060.48 (nearest penny)
b £222.48 (nearest penny)

3 £297.60

4 £84.21 (nearest penny)

Indices, page 23

1
a 36   b 125   c 17
d 24   e 5625   f 15625
g 390625 h 1   i $\frac{1}{16}$

2
a 2.2×10^4 b 4.6×10^{-2}
c 3.92×10^{10} d 5.924×10^{-5}
e 7×10^8 f 2.75×10^6

3 a 5×10^8 b 1.48×10^{22} c 6.093×10^{-12}

4 a 4×10^{16} b 2×10^8

Practice questions

1 a i 7.348×10^8
    ii 5.7×10^{-4} (2)
b i 2.02122×10^{-6}
  ii 6.30×10^{-11} (3 sf)   (4)

2 a £1054   (3)   b 7%   (2)

3 a 60%   (1)
b 66%, $\frac{2}{3}$, 0.67, 0.7   (2)
c i $1\frac{1}{6}$ (1)
  ii 2   (1)
  iii $7\frac{1}{2}$ (1)

4 a
```
    312
  × 67
  -----
  18720
   2184
  -----
  £20904    (3)
```
b $70 \times £300$ (2)

Algebra

Patterns in numbers, page 26

1 a 8, 16, 24, 32, 40, 48
b $8n$
c 800

2 a $60 - 5n$ b 10   c 13th term

3 a ◁▷◁ b 3 5 7 9   c $2n + 1$

101

page 27

1. (1) **a** $n^2 + 2n + 1$ **b** $n^2 + 3n - 2$
   c $2n^2 + n + 4$ **d** $4n^2 + 2n + 3$
   (2) **a** 36 **b** 38
   c 59 **d** 113

2. **a** 6 19 38 63 **b** 339

3. **a** 6 19 42 75 **b** 483

Use of algebra, page 28

1. **a** $4h$ **b** $4a + 7b$ **c** $11xy$ **d** $4x^2$
2. **a** $42t^2$ **b** $60f^2g$
3. **a** $3w + 6$ **b** $-4c^2 - 24$
   c $5a^2 - 10a + 45$ **d** $k^2 + 8k$
   e $2mn - m^2$

page 30

1. **a** $6x^2 - x - 12$
   b $5y^2 - 16y + 12$
   c $2x^2y^2 + 15xy + 28$

2. **a** $(x + 2)(x + 3)$
   b $(x + 4)(x - 2)$
   c $(x - 5)(x - 1)$

3. **a** $(x - 3)(x + 3)$
   b $(r - 13)(r + 13)$
   c $(a - b)(a + b)$

4. **a** $x = \dfrac{3y - 2z}{4}$ **b** $x = 5t + s$
   c $x = \dfrac{s^2 - t}{4}$

Graphs of straight lines, page 33

1. **a** 2 **b** 2 **c** 1
2. **a** 2 **b** -1 **c** -3
3. **a** -3 **b** 2 **c** 5
4. **a** Yes **b** Yes **c** No
5. **a** Linear **b** Not linear **c** Linear
6. **a** **b** 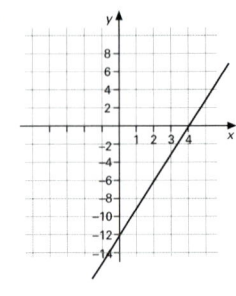 **c**

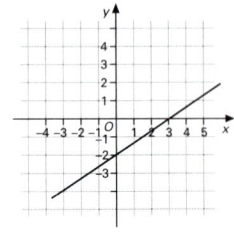

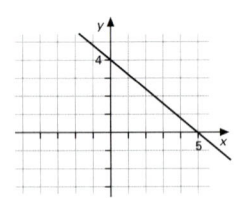

Practical graphs, page 36

1. 4.45 hours
2. 20.83 km/h

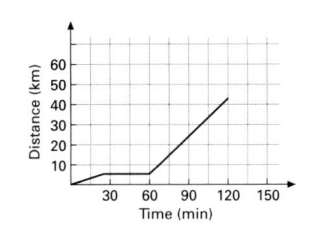

3.

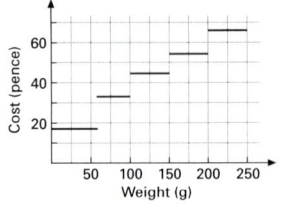

4.
   a 24€ 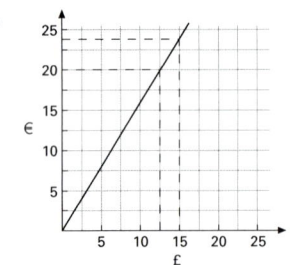
   b £12.50

5.

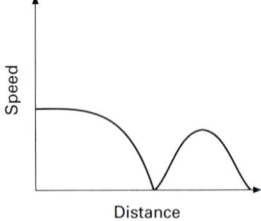

Solving equations, page 39

1. **a** $x = 5$ **b** $x = 5.5$ **c** $x = 12.5$

2. **a** $x = 3$ $y = 1$
   b $x = 2$ $y = 4$
   c $x = 3$ $y = 5$

3. **a** $x = -2$ or $x = -6$
   b $x = -6$ or $x = 8$
   c $x = -3$ or $x = 9$

4. **a** 14.6 or -14.6 **b** 6.4 **c** 5.43

Curved graphs, page 43

1. 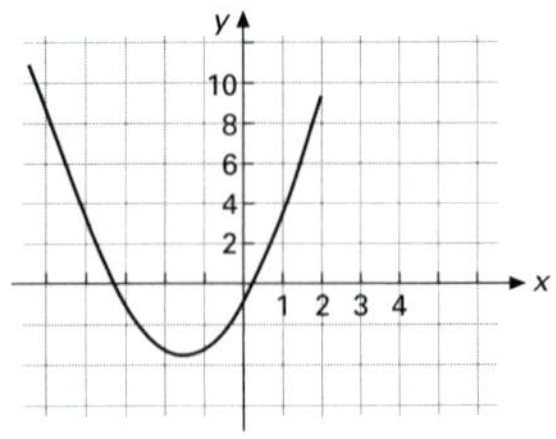
2. 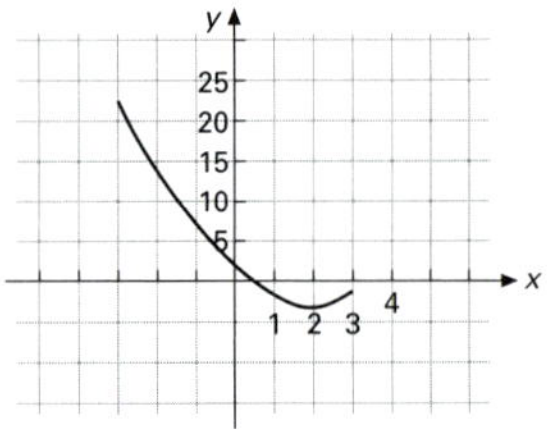
3. **a**

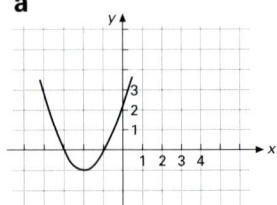

4. **a** $x = -1$ or $x = 5$
   b $x = 1$ or $x = -3$
   c $x = 1.2$ or $x = 4.8$
   d $x = 2.3$ or $x = 0.2$

Inequalities, page 44

1 a [number line with closed circle at 4, arrow right]
b [number line with open circle at −3, arrow left]
c [number line closed at 1, open at 6]
d [number line open at −5, open at −3]
e [number line closed at −4, closed at 2]

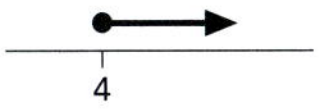

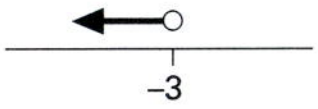

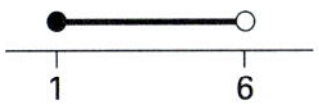

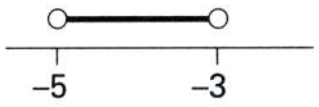

2 a $x > 1.5$
b $x < \frac{5}{3}$
c $x \geq 2.5$
d $x < 1$
e $x \leq -1$

page 45

1 a $-2 \leq x \leq 2$
b $x \leq -4$ or $x \geq 4$
c $x \leq -8$ or $x \geq 8$
d $-1 < x < 1$

2 a, b, 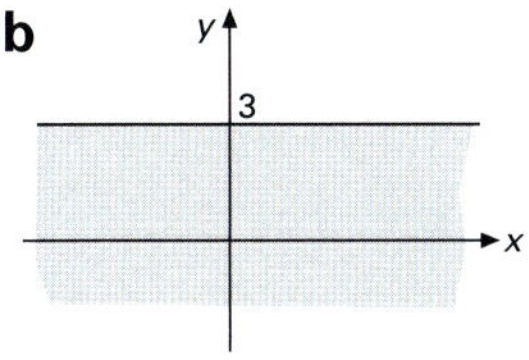 c, 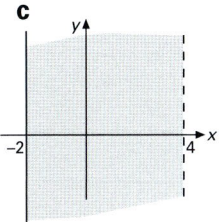 d [inequality region graphs]

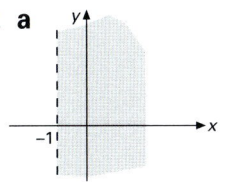

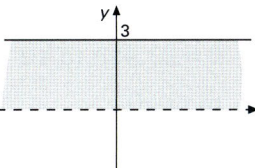

page 46

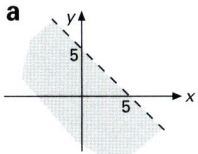

1 a, b, 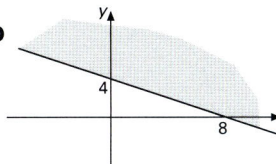 c, 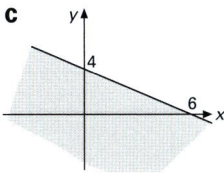 d [inequality region graphs]

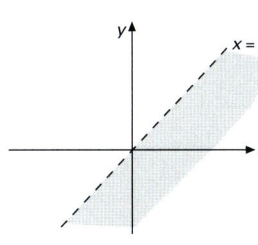

2 a, 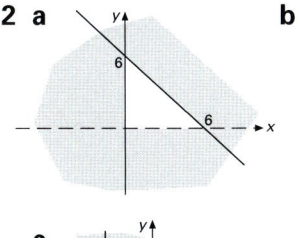 b, 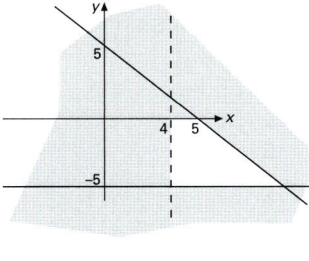 c [inequality region graphs]

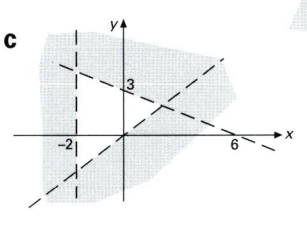

Practice questions

1 a i 29   **ii** $4n - 3$ (2)   **b** $(4n - 3)^2$ (1)

2 a [graph of Volume (litres) vs Time (mins), curve rising from 0 to 100] (4)

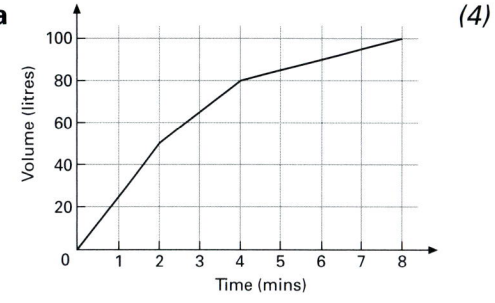

b 12.5 litres   (2)

3 a $y = x + 2$ (2)   **c** $x = \frac{10}{3}$, $y = \frac{4}{3}$ (2)

4 a $n > \frac{1}{5}$ (3)   **b** $2x^2 + 5x - 3$ (2)

c $(x + 1)(x - 4)$ (2)   **d** $t = \sqrt{\dfrac{2s}{g}}$ (2)

5 a

Pattern	No. Circles	No. Stars
4	5	16
5	6	25

(4)

b i 21   (1)   **ii** 400   (2)
c 64   (2)
d i $n + 1$ (1)   **ii** n^2 (1)

6 a $x < 4$ (5)   **b** $x = -4$ (4)

7 a $4^3 - 22(4) + 24 = 0$ (2)
b 1.2   (3)   **c** −5.2   (1)

8 a $x \leq 1$
b i $x \geq -1.4$ (2)   **ii** −1   (1)

Shape and space

Transformations, page 52

1 a, b, c [tessellation diagrams of triangles, trapeziums, hexagons]

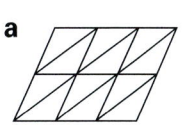

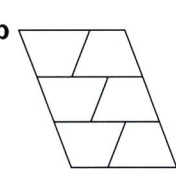

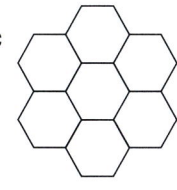

2 a $\begin{pmatrix} 3 \\ -2 \end{pmatrix}$ **b** $\begin{pmatrix} 1 \\ 2 \end{pmatrix}$ **c** $\begin{pmatrix} 7 \\ -2 \end{pmatrix}$ **d** $\begin{pmatrix} -5 \\ -2 \end{pmatrix}$

page 54

1 a,b

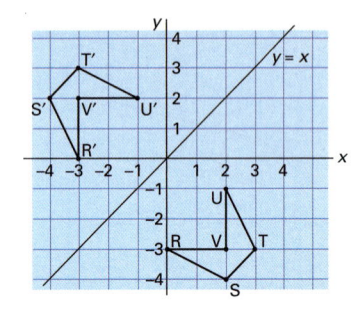

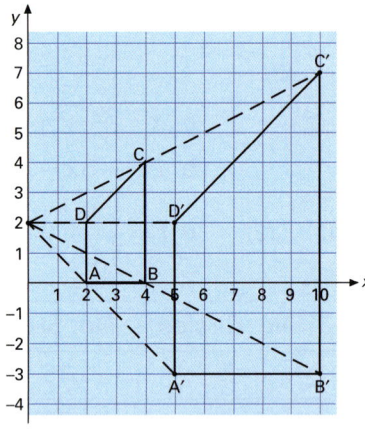

2 a,b

c Scale factor of inverse is $\frac{2}{5}$

3 a,b

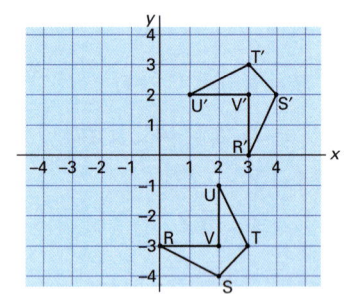

c Rotation 90° clockwise about the origin

page 55

1 a CÂB = EÂD (common angle)
ACB = AÊD (corresponding angles, parallel lines)
so ABC = ADE (angle sum of a triangle = 180°)
so the triangles ABC and ADE have three equal angles and are similar

b Scale factor from large triangle to small triangle = $\frac{2}{5}$

so $\frac{y}{y+4} = \frac{2}{5}$

$5y = 2y + 8$
$3y = 8$ so $y = 2\frac{2}{3}$ cm.

$\frac{x+3}{x} = \frac{5}{2}$

$2x + 6 = 5x$
$6 = 3x$ so $x = 4.5$ cm.

2 a,b,c

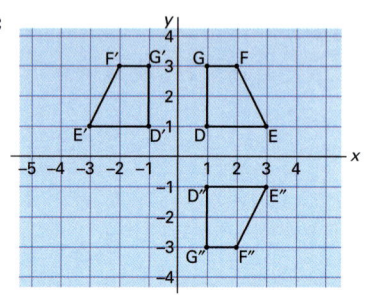

d Reflection in the x axis

Trigonometry, page 56

1 a $a = 32°$
b $b = 55°$
c $c = 54°$

2 a $d = 64.2$ cm (3 sf)
b $e = 1020$ km (3 sf)
c $f = 5.09$ m.

page 57

1 0.409 m (3 sf)

2 14.3 km (3 sf)

3 a BC = 27 m (isosceles triangle)
b AB = 29.4 m (3 sf)

4 129 m (3 sf)

Units of measurement, p. 58

1 a 400 cm
b 6200 m
c 8.5 cm
d 7.8 km
e 4.8 g
f 2900 mg
g 94 t
h 5850 g
i 0.45 ℓ
j 2.3 ℓ
k 250 cℓ
l 450 mℓ

2 a 2 ft
b 144 ins
c 90 ft
d $3\frac{1}{3}$ yds
e 3 miles
f 8800 yds
g 160 oz
h $1\frac{1}{2}$ lbs
i 70 lbs
j $3\frac{1}{2}$ st
k $2\frac{1}{2}$ gal
l 12 gal

page 59

1 a 10 cm
b 5 ft
c 10 miles
d 24 in
e 120 g
f 2 lb
g 65 kg
h 8 oz
i 3000 ℓ
j 27 ℓ
k 4 pt
l 20 gal

2 a Accept 2 m to 3 m
b Accept 2 m to 3 m
c Accept 2 to 5 lbs
d Accept 30 to 80 g
e Accept 0.4 ℓ to 1 ℓ

Perimeter and circumference, page 60

1 a 1.5 m **b** 6.5 m

2 a 78.5 cm (1 dp)
   b 17.0 m (1 dp)
   c 17.0 cm (1 dp)

page 61

1 a 6.37 cm (3 sf) **b** 87.9 m (3 sf)

2 a 1.11 mm (3 sf) **b** 0.420 km (3 sf)

3 a 5.91 m (3 sf) **b** 114 cm (3 sf)

Pythagoras, page 62

1 a 20.8 m (3 sf) **b** 3.45 m (3 sf)

2 a 56.6 cm (3 sf) **b** $6\frac{1}{2}$ km

page 63

1 a 55.4 cm **b** 6 km

2 a 4.47 cm **b** 2r = 6.71 m (3 sf)
                so r = 3.35 m (3 sf)

Areas, nets and surface areas, page 66

1 a 3.68 m² **b** 11.7 m²
   c 22.05 m² **d** 17.5 m²

2 a 72.4 m² **b** 82 m²

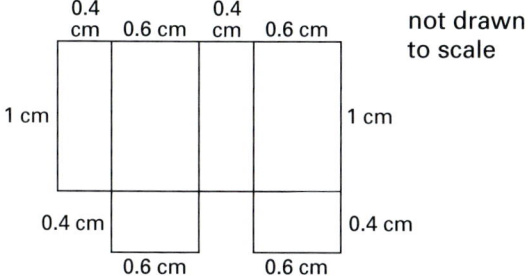

3 a, b, 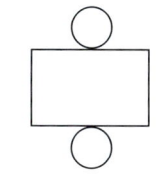 c, 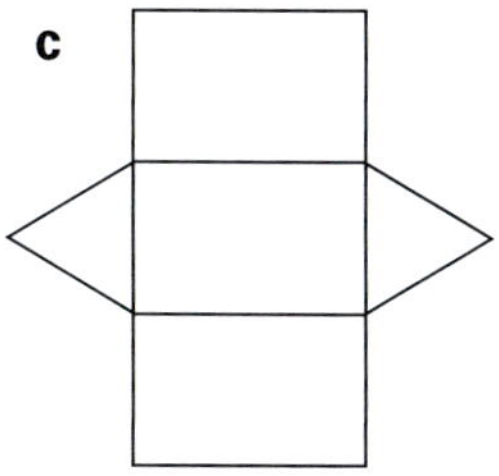 d (nets)

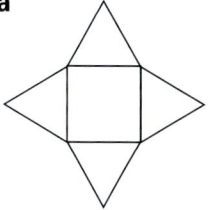

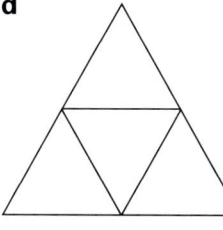

4 (diagram, not drawn to scale)

5 (isometric drawing of cuboid 5 cm × 2 cm × 4 cm)

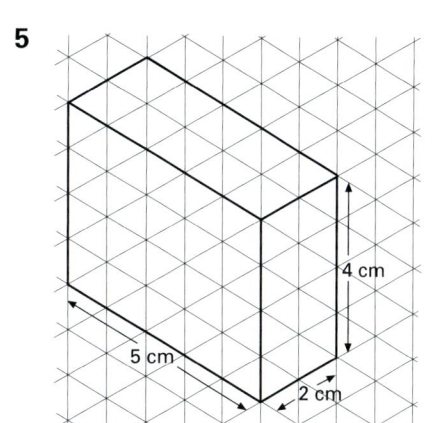

page 67

1 972 m²

2 a 4 cm² **b** 80 cm² **c** 120 000 cm²

3 a 2 m² **b** 8 000 000 m² **c** 450 000 m²

Angles, page 68

1 a 35° **b** 82° **c** 125°
   d 155° **e** 145° **f** 98°
   g 55° **h** 25°

2 a 45°, b 78°, c 120°, d 143°, e 105°, f 171°, g 270°, h 230°

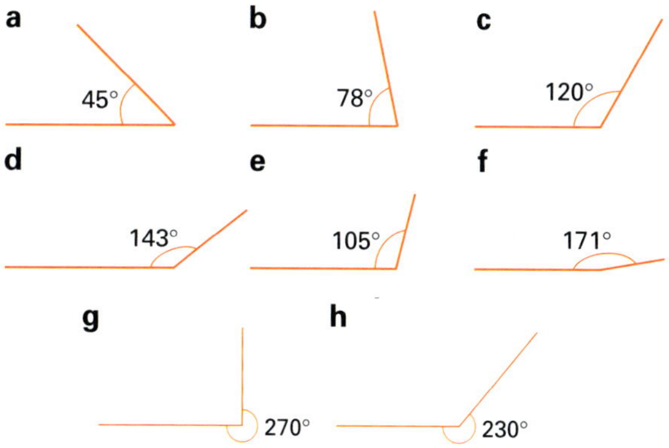

page 69

1 a a = 99° **e** e = 72° **g** i = 99°
   b b = 77° f = 108° **h** j = 130°
   c c = 23° g = 108° k = 20°
   d d = 85° **f** h = 55°

page 71

1 a a = 73° (vertically opposite angles)
     b = 73° (corresponding angles)

   b c = 45° (external angle of regular octagon)
     d = 135° (internal angle of regular octagon
          = 180 − external angle)

   c e = 73° (isosceles triangle, radii are equal)
     f = 34° (angle sum of triangle = 180°)

   d g = 62° (vertically opposite angles)
     h = 118° (interior angles)
     i = 62° (corresponding angles)

2 a 078°   **b** 258°

3

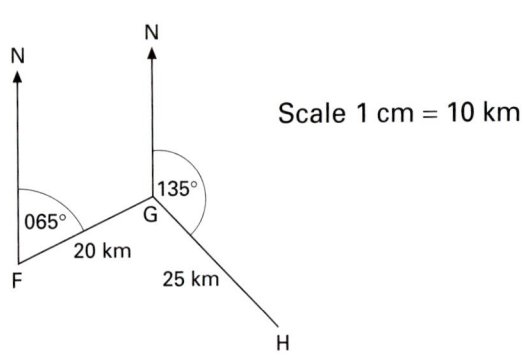

Scale 1 cm = 10 km

a 37.0 km (3 sf) (Allow 36 to 38 km)
b 104° (Allow 103 to 106°)

Volume, page 73

1 a 262.14 cm³   **b** 50.40 m³

2 a Height of triangle = 1.658 m (4 sf)
   Area of triangle = 1.161 m² (4 sf)
   Volume of prism = 4.88 m³ (3 sf)

b Area of circle = 4.155 m² (4 sf)
   Volume of cylinder = 16.6 m³ (3 sf)

3 Volume of piece removed = 4.428 m³
   Volume of shape without piece removed = 30.996 m³
   Volume of shape = 26.568 m³

4 40 cm³

5 1500 kg/m³

Dimensional analysis, page 74

1 a length
  b volume
  c area
  d volume
  e area

2 a is not a length area or volume. This is because the first term of the expression is a volume, whereas the second term is an area.

Symmetry, page 75

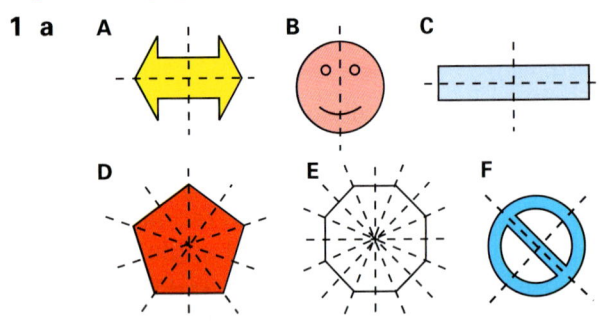

1 a A   B   C
      D   E   F

b A 2   B 1   C 2
    D 5   E 8   F 2

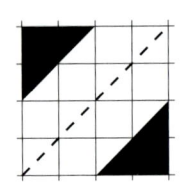

2

3 a

b

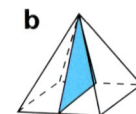

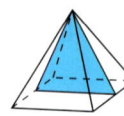

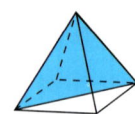

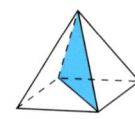

Loci, page 71

1

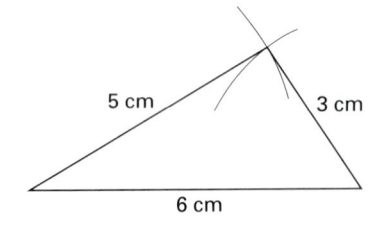

5 cm   3 cm
   6 cm

Angles are: 30° 94° 56°

2 Scale 1 cm = 2 km

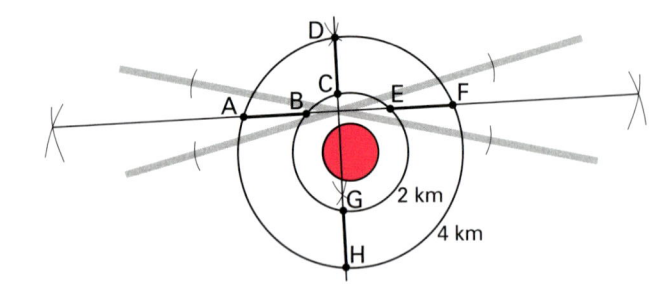

2 km
4 km

The telephone mast can lie on any of the line segments AB, CD, EF or GH

Practice questions

1 a Rotation 90° anticlockwise about the origin (3)
  b Reflection in the line $y = x$ (2)
  c

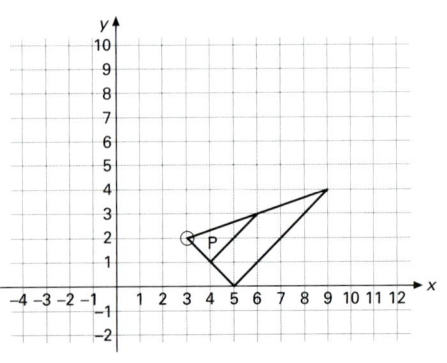

(2)

2 a Isosceles   (1)   **b** 80°   (2)

106

Handling data

Dealing with data, page 81

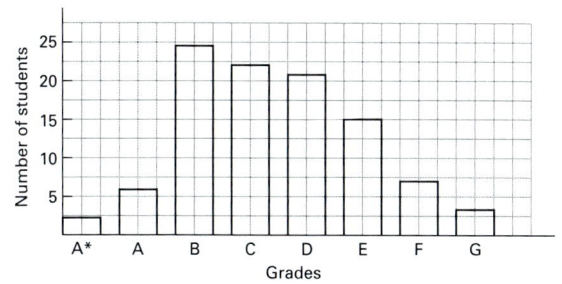

1 a [bar chart: Number of students vs Grades A*–G]

b 54% **c** B

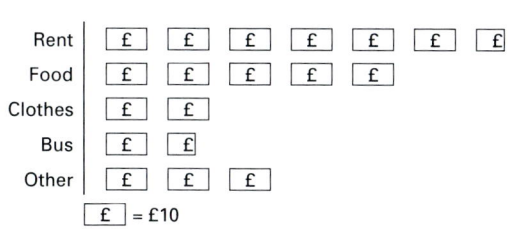

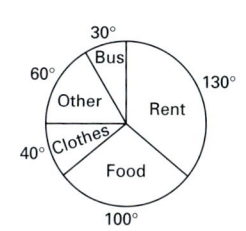

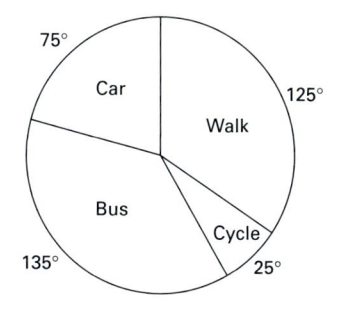

2 [pictogram: Rent 7, Food 5, Clothes 2, Bus 2, Other 3; £ = £10]

3 [pie chart: Bus 30°, Rent 130°, Food 100°, Clothes 40°, Other 60°]

4 [pie chart: Car 75°, Walk 125°, Cycle 25°, Bus 135°]

page 84

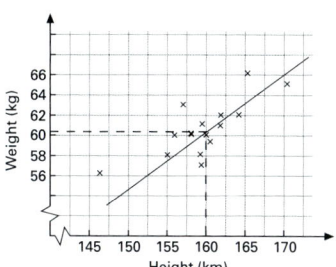

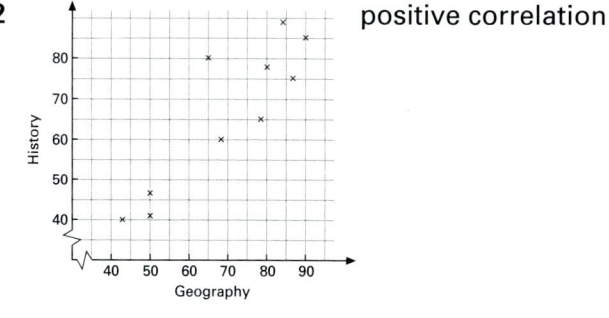

1 a [scatter graph of Weight vs Height] **c** 60.5 kg

2 [scatter graph History vs Geography] positive correlation

Averages, page 87

	a	b
1 mean	6	19
median	6.5	18
mode	7	16

2 a 3.2125 **b** 4 **c** 3

3 mean 3.4, modal group $0 \leq t \leq 2$ mins

Comparing data, page 90

	mean	IQR
1 John	3.16	1
Martin	2.3	4

John has higher mean and lower IQR

	mean	IQR
2 a	13	8
b	12	8

3 Median 35.5 IQR 16

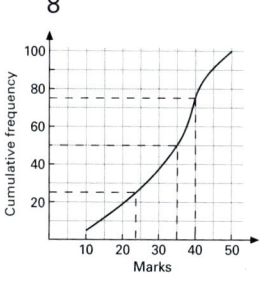

[cumulative frequency graph]

Simple probability, page 93

1 Fair, 3 prime numbers, 3 numbers not prime

2 a $\frac{1}{6}$ **b** $\frac{1}{3}$ **c** 1

3 a
Score	1	2	3	4	5	6
Rel. freq.	0.12	0.14	0.25	0.20	0.14	0.15

b 150

Laws of probability, page 94

1 0.08 **2 a** $\frac{1}{12}$ **b** $\frac{1}{4}$

Tree diagrams, page 95

1 a 0.6 **b** 0.2 **2 b** $\frac{3}{5}$ **c** $\frac{7}{20}$

page 97

1 a $\frac{4}{25}$ **b** $\frac{6}{25}$ **2 a** 0.51 **b** 0.67

Practice Questions

1 a 1 *(1)* **b** 1.5 *(3)* **c** 1.8 *(3)*

2 a [scatter graph Pulse rate vs Age] *(2)(1)*

b strong positive *(1)* **d** 96 *(1)*

3 a i 0.1 *(1)* **ii** 0.4 *(1)* **iii** 0.6 *(1)*

b 6 *(2)*

4 b $\frac{4}{15}$ *(2)*

107